PRACTICAL
QUILLING

PRACTICAL QUILLING

ANNE REDMAN

Kangaroo Press

ACKNOWLEDGMENTS

I would like to thank my husband Errol, my sons Nick, Alex, Matt and Michael, and my parents, Les and Tricia Fossey, for their constant support and encouragement as I have worked on this book, with a special thanks to Mum, a fellow quiller, who has been my 'technical sounding board' throughout. I would also like to thank all those subscribers to Australian Quiller's Quarterly who sent in designs for consideration—without you, this book would never have been finished. A special thanks to Meg Prance, who always had another design just forming to fill any gap I found.

PRACTICAL QUILLING

First published in Australia in 1998 by Kangaroo Press
an imprint of Simon & Schuster (Australia) Pty Limited
20 Barcoo Street, East Roseville NSW 2069

A Viacom Company
Sydney New York London

© Anne Redman 1998

National Library of Australia
Cataloguing-in-Publication data

Redman, Anne.
Practical quilling.

ISBN 0 86417 944 8.

1. Paper quillwork. I. Title.
745.54

Set in Sabon 10/12
Printed in China through Colorcraft Ltd., Hong Kong

9 8 7

Contents

FOREWORD

'Quilling?' people ask. 'What's that?' I sometimes wish the name had been left as paper filigree, but the craft is so much more than that now.

I was originally introduced to quilling at a craft show in the mid 1980s. I found it an easy craft to do with a young baby in tow. I could leave things and come back when I had more time, and it didn't cost the earth to set myself up: quilling paper and tool, blank cards or cardboard and some PVA glue, along with a little imagination. In fact, $20 would give you a pretty good selection of supplies.

In 1992 I heard of a new publication called the *Australian Quiller's Quarterly*, and I felt it was time to explore new ideas with my quilling, so I joined. The newsletter, which of course comes out quarterly, is not only a source of new designs, both easy and challenging, but also a wealth of ideas and tips to do with quilling.

Each newsletter has a theme with subscribers submitting designs. I even won the occasional prize for my designs.

Anne Redman was founding editor and is now patron of the *AQQ*. She is now taking us (the subscribers) on a new adventure—our own book. It contains a selection of designs for beginners through to the more experienced quiller, which have been designed by a wide range of subscribers from around Australia. (Their potted biographies appear on page 8.)

Quilling is for everyone, no matter your age or sex—all you need is a little corner and some time. We hope you have a lot of fun exploring quilling through our book.

Trina Hawkins
Upper Brookfield
Queensland

INTRODUCTION

Dear fellow quillers,
Some years ago I started a business selling blank craft cards. As the business grew, I was looking for new lines, and someone mentioned quilling. I was so ignorant of this craft that I tried looking it up in the dictionary, but was none the wiser! Then I saw a demonstration at a craft show, and a client kindly gave me a few basic ideas. From there, I simply played with the raw materials myself. I was delighted with the simplicity of this craft, and in no time at all found I was producing my own designs.

Quilling is a wonderful craft because the techniques can be mastered at any age. I have know children as young as five to be able to make simple designs, yet also know many grandparents who are still quilling well into their retirement years. It can also be mastered by people who can't manage the techniques of other crafts. For example, I know several ladies who suffer from arthritis, and one delightful lady with MS, who all manage to quill. I also know of a child who had fine motor skill problems, but was thrilled with the work he could produce when quilling (it was a great

exercise for him too). Quilling is also an inexpensive craft, and extremely practical—everyone gives cards.

Through my business I came in touch with quillers from all around Australia, and most seemed to be on a constant quest for new designs. Yet most had some designs of their own too. I soon formulated a solution for everyone, and so began the *Australian Quiller's Quarterly* newsletter, which aimed to share ideas and foster the craft within Australia. I no longer have my business, and am no longer the editor of *AQQ*, but was delighted to take on the honorary title of Patron. Published four times a year, *AQQ* has a group of staunch supporters, many of whom comment that it is more like getting a letter from a friend than a publication. It seemed an obvious extension of our work with *AQQ* to put together a book of designs by our subscribers.

I hope you enjoy our book. Until next time, Happy Quilling

Anne Redman

LIST OF CONTRIBUTORS

Jessie Beacom from Sydney's Punchbowl has been quilling for four years. Jessie mainly quills cards for family and friends.

Maureen Bowden from Kirrawee in New South Wales has been quilling for five or six years. She has taught many classes, and along with several students has won prizes for her work.

Moya Burns is a great-grandma from Redcliffe in Brisbane. Moya began quilling after she was given a quilled birthday card—she hasn't stopped since.

Christine Dicks lives on a farm in Queensland's Darling Downs, and has been quilling for six years. Chris loves both teaching and designing quilling.

Elizabeth Dicks is a young mother from Tara in south Queensland who 'lives for craft'; she has been quilling for seven years.

Nancy Evans is from Baulkham Hills in Sydney, and has been quilling for four years. She meets regularly with local quilling groups, and has won an award for her quilling.

Tricia Fossey is a grandma from Greenslopes, Brisbane, who has been quilling for seven years. Tricia enjoys passing on her skills to anyone who will have a go.

Jill Garsia is a grandma from Bribie Island, Queensland, and has been quilling for six years. Jill gives demonstrations and holds classes.

Norma Genn is a great-grandma from MacGregor in Brisbane. Norma loves to make cards for family and friends.

Eleanor Georpalidis is a young mum who lives in Baulkham Hills, New South Wales.

Margery Hamer is grandma who lives near Gympie in Queensland. Margery has been quilling for about six years, and also enjoys cake decorating and painting.

Trina Hawkins is from Upper Brookfield in Brisbane's west. Trina has been quilling for ten years, and has taught quilling for years, especially to children's groups.

Enid Kenny lives in Toowoomba, Queensland. Enid taught herself to quill from a book, and now loves to design too.

Betty Kowald is a great-grandma from Birdwood, South Australia. She learnt to quill at a craft morning ten years ago, and enjoys teaching quilling.

Lynne Mayes is a grandma from Rainbow Flat in New South Wales, who first saw quilling eighteen years ago, and became 'hooked'.

Christine Meston is from Jamboree Heights in Brisbane. Christine has taught many crafts, and has been quilling for so long she can't remember when or how she started!

Ellen McCartney-Lees began quilling five years ago when she bought a kit. Today her life revolves around quilling. With her husband Mike, Ellen is joint editor of *AQQ* and runs a quilling supply business; they attend craft shows, give classes and demonstrations, and can supply just about any colour paper you could wish for.

Desley Mole is a mum from Brisbane who has been quilling for over five years. Desley has taught Adult Education classes, and currently enjoys quilling to frame.

Licia Politis is a mum from Como, Sydney, who has been quilling for eight years. Licia has taught several others, and particularly enjoyed teaching at her daughter's school.

Lorraine Poltock is a mum from Park Ridge in Brisbane. Lorraine enjoys many different crafts.

Meg Prance is from Blacktown in Sydney, and has been quilling for five years. Inspired by *AQQ* to begin designing, Meg teaches a regular class in her area, and has won several prizes for her work.

Anne Redman from Middle Park in Brisbane, first tried quilling eight years ago, in association with her supply business, and was the creator and founding editor of the *Australian Quiller's Quarterly*. Anne has had several designs published in magazines and books, and has taught quilling to groups from Adult Education down to grade 3.

Rosa Robartson is from Merredin, Western Australia, and has been quilling for eight years. Rosa learnt to quill so she could teach her daughter, but found herself totally hooked instead.

Kerry Schemioneck is from Charleville in Queensland, and has been quilling for four years. As well as gifts for family and friends, Kerry has sold quite a bit of her work.

Audrey Sheffield is from Townsville in Queensland, and has been quilling for three years. Audrey enjoys teaching quilling, and watching others create their own designs.

Eileen Stephenson is a great-grandma from Liverpool in Sydney who has been quilling for four years. Eileen regularly attends quillers' meetings.

Marilyn Sullivan is from Lara in Victoria, and has been quilling for five years. Marilyn has taught quilling to a children's group and enjoys making cards for all occasions.

Heather Tathem is a student from Mt Gravatt in Brisbane, and has been quilling for six years. Heather taught some fellow students to quill, and they made items for their school fete.

Glenys Thompson is a working mum from Whyalla Playford, South Australia, and has been quilling for five years. Glenys has taught quilling at her local craft group.

Wendy Verity is from Leumeah, New South Wales, and has been quilling for eight years. Self-taught, Wendy has taught many classes herself, and has won several prizes for her work.

Annette Wann is a nursing sister and mum from Thornlands, Brisbane, and has been quilling for three years. Annette likes to combine stamping with her quilling.

Clare Waterworth is a mum from Mt Gravatt, Brisbane. Clare is self-taught, and has had some of her work featured in a magazine.

Marilyn Whitfield is from New Farm in Brisbane, and taught herself to quill six years ago. Marilyn has organised quillers' meetings, and loves teaching the craft to others.

For more information about the *Australian Quiller's Quarterly* newsletter, or for information on quilling supplies, contact Ellen and Mike at:

Quilling by Ellen
PO Box 352
Jimboomba
Queensland 4280
Phone: (07) 55 463 753
Fax: (07) 44 463 941
E-mail: quilling@fan.net.au

15mm: $^1/_{16}$"; 3mm: $^1/_8$"; 6mm: $^1/_4$"; 9mm: $^3/_8$"; 12mm: 1"; 15mm: $^3/_8$"; 20mm: $^3/_4$"; 25mm: 1"; 30mm: $1^1/_4$"; 40mm: $1^5/_8$"

MATERIALS

THE TOOL

There are several different tools available on the market; which one you choose is simply a case of personal preference. However, I would recommend you dodge those that are made of moulded plastic as they tend to have a very short 'pin', and it is difficult to roll some papers onto them. Most Australian made tools have a wooden handle with a metal pin of some type attached in one end. My tool has a fine metal pin with a slot down one side. Some dedicated quillers use only a round toothpick or hat pin. Cost of a standard quilling tool should be around $2–$3.

PAPERS

There is a delightful range of colours available in precut papers. Most work is done in paper 3 mm wide, but some dedicated quillers like to use 1.5 mm papers. There is no doubt that the finished product is much finer, and looks very delicate, but it is also harder to work with, and definitely not the place to start. You will also find 6 mm and 9 mm wide papers available, used to make roses and fringed flowers (as described on pages 14–15). Strips are generally made in 30 cm lengths, though a few companies do make them 60 cm long. Many quillers work with pieces that are fractions of 30 cm. So, you will often find 30 cm, 15 cm (1/2 strip), 10 cm (1/3 strip), 7.5 cm (1/4 strip) or 3–4 cm (1/8 strip) used in designs. If you always fold and tear your strips into even measurements, there is never any waste.

The other type of paper you will find in the craft shops is candle paper—it is usually 25 or 40 mm wide, and is used specifically for making candles (it comes in very handy for Christmas and birthdays). The candle paper I use is only 10 cm long.

GLUE

You will need a good quality white PVA glue which will dry clear. The only difficulty in using it is that it can leave a shiny spot on your card if you use too much or make a mistake. Glue is best applied with a toothpick; finished rolls can be dipped in glue using tweezers, then positioned on the card.

MISCELLANEOUS

Your remaining materials are the type of things you should find around home:
* scissors
* tweezers (fine point are best)
* a tray for glue (e.g. plastic lid)
* toothpicks (to apply glue)
* ruler
* cards or gift tags (may be cut from sheets of cardboard to begin with)
* marker pens
* you may also find some use for ribbons, beads/pearls, sequin waste, lace and even leaves, twigs, gumnuts and so on

I often find that a few extras make a design just that little bit special and different—they can be added to a design, or used in place of a quilled piece.

Materials for quilling

THE QUILLING BOARD

If you wish to work a design where symmetry is important, or you are making jewellery, Christmas decorations or some other free-standing item, a quilling board will be an invaluable asset. Although there will be times that you won't really need it, it is always good to have a smooth, clean surface to work on. The great thing is that you can make one yourself for very little cost, and may even find you already have all the required materials. A quilling board is made of three layers:

Layer 1: Either corrugated cardboard or polystyrene foam; about 20 cm (8") square would be a reasonable size. You will be pushing pins into this, so it needs to be fairly thick. You may choose to use two or three layers to give a good thick board.

Layer 2: Paper marked with 1 cm (½") squares (also makes a handy built-in ruler). Mark a stronger central line both horizontally and vertically (to help keep your pattern even). This is all that is necessary, but there are a few other things you may like to mark on your paper:

✳ A series of circles or ovals centred over the cross. You may even like to divide these circles into five, six or more segments like a pie. The type of design you use will determine the markings you will need.

✳ If you are working on a symmetrical design for a box lid, you may like to trace the lid shape.

Much of this will mean nothing to you if you are just starting out, but refer back to these ideas as you work through increasingly more involved designs. It is always easy to make another board if you need a few more things marked on it.

Layer 3: Gladbake or clear Contact—PVC glue will adhere to this, but not permanently. At the most it will require a knife slid underneath to gently lift your finished piece.

Free assembling using the quilling board

When using your board, rather than gluing quilled pieces to the surface (as is the case when attaching a design to a card), you glue them to each other where they touch. Pieces assembled in this manner are said to be 'free assembled'. Pins are pushed into the board to hold pieces in place while the glue dries. If you find that some pieces stick to the board, simply run a knife under the completed, dry design to lift.

OPTION

Many quillers become concerned because their rolls never seem to turn out the same size. While I can see that this is frustrating, I wouldn't worry too much, as I feel this is part of the charm of a handmade item. However, if you are concerned about it, there are three solutions. The first is to buy a commercially made quilling board which is covered with a series of circles of different sizes. You drop the loosening roll into the appropriate sized circle, thus limiting how far it can unroll. These boards can be relatively expensive.

The second solution: If you hunt around newsagencies and art shops, you should be able to find a plastic template of circles. You can attach this to a homemade quilling board, and achieve the same result. The third idea is to attach a series of washers from the hardware shop to your board. Both these ideas come from *AQQ* subscribers.

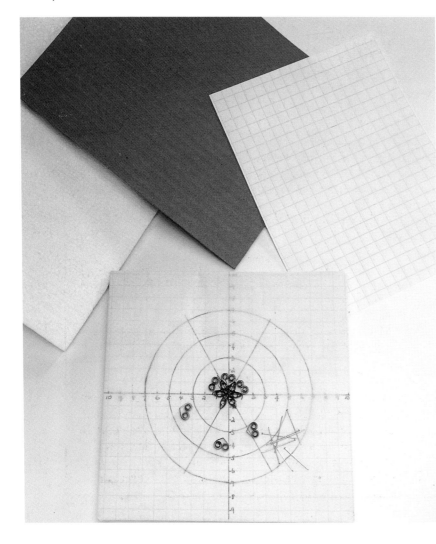

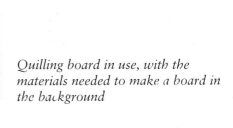

Quilling board in use, with the materials needed to make a board in the background

15mm: ¹⁄₁₆"; 3mm: ¹⁄₈"; 6mm: ¹⁄₄"; 9mm: ³⁄₈"; 12mm: 1"; 15mm: ³⁄₈"; 20mm: ³⁄₄"; 25mm: 1"; 30mm: 1¹⁄₄"; 40mm: 1⁵⁄₈"

TECHNIQUES

BASIC QUILLED SHAPES

Closed rolls

Tight roll		Wind strip onto tool, glue loose end, remove.
Loose roll		Wind strip onto tool. Loosen grip to allow paper to uncoil. Remove from tool and glue loose end. (Note: the more you loosen, the bigger the finished shape will be.)
Teardrop		Make a loose roll. Pinch one end between your thumb and index finger.
Eye		Make a loose roll. Place between thumbs and index fingers of both hands and pinch both ends.
Petal		Make a teardrop. Hold pinched end and twist gently to one side.
Leaf		Make an eye. Hold both ends, twist one end up and the other down.
Heart		Make a teardrop. Hold pinched end, and push in opposite end with finger nail/quilling tool/tweezers.
Semi-circle		Make a teardrop. Pinch other end off-centre. The position of the second pinch will give anything from a long flat semi-circle to a tall thin one.
Oval		Make a loose roll. Push gently into shape, but do not pinch.
Star		Make an eye. While still holding pinched ends, push hands in toward each other, so forcing another pinch in middle of each side.
Tulip		Make an eye. Loosen grip slightly on left end, and push right end back in to form three peaks.
Off-centre teardrops		Make a loose roll. Place it on quilling board. Push a pin into board; place loose roll against it. Place a second pin in centre of roll (don't push into board yet); move it as close to first pin as possible. Secure pin in board. Place a dot of glue between the two pins. Allow to dry. Remove pins, hold glued end and pinch opposite end. (See photo overleaf.)

The off-centre teardrops take a little more work, but for a special project, like jewellery, Christmas decorations, or box lids, they are well worth the extra effort.

There are many variations that can be made from the basic loose roll shape, depending on how you pinch or push.

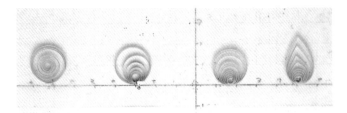

Steps in turning a loose roll into an off-centre teardrop

Bells

Here are two methods. The second is by far the easier, but the first will give better control of the final shape.

1. Dimensional roll		Slip end of paper into tool and turn 2–3 times, adding a spot of glue to secure. Continue rolling, but gradually move the paper further up the tool to achieve a bell shape. Add a little glue every few turns to keep secure, glue off loose end.
2. Bell		Make a tight roll. Push over sharpened end of pencil or special tool to give bell shape, adjusting slightly if desired. Smear glue inside bell, allow to dry.
Bell hammer		There are 3 methods of making a bell hammer: 1. Make small bell shape using 5 cm (2") paper; glue small end in bell. 2. Using 3 cm strip, wind all but 5 mm onto tool—glue to hold. Glue 'tail' in bell. 3. Make 3 cm tight roll and glue on front edge of bell.

Leaf options

Here are two methods. The second is by far the easier, but the first will give better control of the final shape.

Cut folded leaves		Fold a piece of 9 mm wide paper in half lengthwise. Cut half leaf shape on fold. Partially unfold, and apply glue on crease—this gives a 3-D leaf, rather than something flat and lifeless. This is the method used to make holly leaves.
Fringed leaves		Made in same manner as cut folded leaves, but before cutting out leaf shape, fringe (see next page) on open edge at an angle of approximately 45°.
Looped leaves		Using a piece of 3 mm paper 5–20 mm long, fold strip over halfway, bring ends together and glue. Bring fold and glued ends together, glue again.

15mm: ¹/₁₆"; 3mm: ¹/₈"; 6mm: ¹/₄"; 9mm: ³/₈"; 12mm: 1"; 15mm: ³/₈"; 20mm: ³/₄"; 25mm: 1"; 30mm: 1¹/₄"; 40mm: 1⁵/₈"

Scrolls—open rolls

When making these shapes, the loose end is not glued down. Shapes can all be varied by rolling more or less of the strip onto your tool.

Scroll		Curl part of a strip around tool, remove.
Double scroll		Fold strip in half, roll each end to left or right. This shape can be varied by folding off-centre, so giving a larger roll on one end, or rolling more on one end than the other.
V-scroll		Fold strip in half, roll each end out.
Heart scroll		Fold strip in half, roll each end in.
S-scroll		Roll top end to one side, bottom to the other. This again can be done unevenly, so one end is larger than the other.
C-scroll		Roll both top and bottom in the same direction.
Spiral		Wind paper in a spiral around and down a round toothpick, skewer or fine knitting needle. Hold for a short time, then release. If you have trouble with this shape staying in place on card, apply a little glue to both top and bottom.

FRINGING

Lengths of fringed paper can be used for many different purposes, but most commonly to make flowers like chrysanthemums or carnations. To fringe a strip of paper (usually 6 mm or 9 mm wide), a series of small cuts are made along one side (see diagram 1).

Cuts should be as close together as possible. It is possible to fold the strip in half first, and so cut two pieces at a time, but you need very sharp scissors to ensure crisp cutting. There is a fringing tool available that makes very neat and even cuts, but it is imported from America, and is quite expensive. You would need to be doing a lot of fringing to justify the expense. Some craft shops are known to hire out fringers (refundable deposit and daily hiring charge); this may be worth checking out, or even suggesting at your local craft shop.

Fringed flowers

See photo overleaf.

Basic flower: Fringe 30 cm x 9 mm or 15 cm x 6 mm, roll into a tight roll. Dip bottom in glue and invert until dry. Fan out fringed edge.

Flower with centre: Fringe a length of 6 mm or 9 mm paper. Glue 5 cm x 3 mm in a contrasting colour to one end (diagram 2). Roll from 3 mm end. Finish as for basic flower.

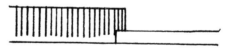

Diagram 2

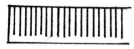

Diagram 1

Diagram 3

More advanced ideas:

Type 1: Fringe 7.5 cm x 6 mm and 15 cm x 9 mm in toning colours, join and allow to dry. Starting at join, trim 9 mm fringed edge and gradually, over 10–12 cm, taper back out to 9 mm (diagram 3). Roll from 6 mm end. Finish as for basic flower (you could also add a centre to this flower).

Type 2: Cut up to 15 cm x 6 mm in a mid to dark colour, then the same length in 9 mm, using a slightly lighter shade. Fringe both pieces. Sit 6 mm on top of 9 mm and roll strips together. You will have to trim a little 6 mm off at the end. Finish as for basic flower. This will give some depth to the colour of your flower.

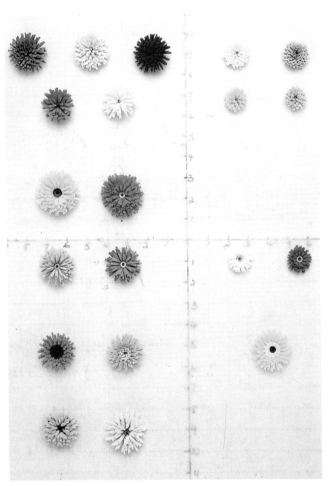

Simple fringed flowers
Row 1 is made from 30 cm strips (left: 9 mm paper, right: 6 mm paper)
Row 2 is made from 15 cm strips (left: 9 mm, right: 6 mm)

Fringed flowers with centres
Row 3 is made from 30 cm strips of 9 mm paper
Row 4 is made from 15 cm strips (left: 9 mm, right: 6 mm)

More advanced fringed flowers
Row 5 shows Type 1 (the flower on the right includes a centre)
Row 6 shows Type 2

ROSES

Folded rose

Folded roses are generally made using 6 mm or 9 mm papers. It is possible to use 3 mm paper, but the wider strips are much easier to use to begin with. Shorter lengths of paper will give a rosebud, longer strips a fuller rose (see photo page 15).

1 Slip end of paper into tool, wind a few rounds and apply a little glue to anchor (diagram 4).

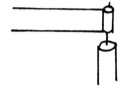

Diagram 4

2 Fold paper towards you and down at a right angle to run parallel to the tool (diagram 5).

3 Roll tool around this angle (diagram 6) until loose end is again out straight (as in diagram 1 again). Do not expect your rose to look much at this stage, and it will not be flat and even like a regular roll.

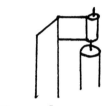

Diagram 5

4 Repeat steps 2 and 3 to end of paper.

5 Remove from tool and loosen. Glue loose end. To secure the centre of your rose, dip the bottom in glue and invert to dry.

Option: Slip tool over peaks on petals and gently bend out.

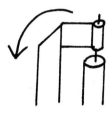

Diagram 6

Trouble shooting: Many new quillers complain that their roses just don't work. Most of the problems occur because the paper has been rolled too tightly. Relax, loosen your grip; it is not important that folds be made at the same distance from the tool, or with any given regularity. But do try to make sure that in step 2 your paper is parallel to the tool.

Spiral rose

If you have difficulty with the standard folded rose, this easy style may solve your problem. I first learned of this type of rose from one of our *AQQ* subscribers. These roses are cut from a circle of coloured paper, so keep your eyes open for any little scraps that look interesting; they don't even have to be single colours—a marbled pattern makes a very effective rose.

You will need a circle 25–30 mm (about 1") in diameter; smaller or larger circles simply give different sized roses, or you can change the width of the spirals to change the height of the rose. These roses will sit flat on your card.

Mark circle with a spiral of 2 or 3 full revolutions as shown in

Diagram 7

15mm: ¹⁄₁₆"; 3mm: ¹⁄₈"; 6mm: ¹⁄₄"; 9mm: ³⁄₈"; 12mm: 1"; 15mm: ³⁄₈"; 20mm: ³⁄₄"; 25mm: 1"; 30mm: 1¹⁄₄"; 40mm: 1⁵⁄₈"

Varieties of roses
TOP LEFT AND RIGHT: **Folded roses** (page 14)
Row 1 is made from 10 cm strips
(left: 9 mm paper, right: 6 mm paper)
Row 2 is made from 15 cm strips
(left: 9 mm paper, right: 6 mm paper)
Row 3 is made from 30 cm strips
(left: 9 mm paper, right: 6 mm paper)

BOTTOM LEFT: **Spiral roses** (page 14)
Row 4, straight cut style
Row 5, wavy cut style

BOTTOM RIGHT:
Row 4, curled roses (page 15)
Row 5, heart punch roses (page 15)

diagram 7. Cut along line in either a straight line or wavy pattern (with practice, pencil marking will not be necessary).

If cutting in a wavy pattern, cut waves as far as possible around the outside, then remove waste (shaded area in diagram 8).

Insert tool at outer end from underneath circle (diagram 9), and roll into centre of circle. Remove tool and glue loose end.

Diagram 8

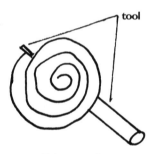

Diagram 9

Curled rose

This is another flower that was featured in *AQQ*, with instructions being sent in by one of our subscribers. They have an advantage over the folded rose in that they sit absolutely flat.

Curled roses can be made either in 9 mm or 6 mm papers, though 6 mm is definitely more fiddly. Instructions here are given for 9 mm, with 6 mm in brackets.

Outer petals (make 5): Cut 1.5 cm x 9 mm (1 cm x 6 mm), curl top corners back (see diagram 10).

Diagram 10

Inner petals (make 5): Cut 1.5 cm x 9 mm (1 cm x 6 mm), and slit half way up from bottom, curl top corners down as for outer petals (diagram 11). Overlap slit pieces and glue—this will give petals depth by raising the curled end.

Diagram 11

Centre: 10 cm x 6 cm (7.5 cm x 3 mm) loose roll.

Option: You can use a small spiral rose for the centre.

To assemble

Join inner petals in a circle, overlapping bottom pieces to form a 'well' in the centre.

Add outer petals underneath, and in gaps between inner petals.

Glue centre into 'well'.

Note: These roses are easier if assembled on a quilling board first. The lines on the board can be used as a guide to keep the petals an even distance apart.

Heart punch rose

You will need a total of 15 heart-shaped petals. Heart punches can be purchased from most craft stores. Rounds as given start at the outside, and work in. Note that hearts overlap a little under halfway (see diagrams).

Round 1: Overlap 5 hearts leaving a small gap at the end. When dry, overlap last two petals to form a cup shape. Use tool to curve tips out and down.

Round 1

Round 2: Overlap 4 hearts, leaving a slightly larger gap at the end. When dry, finish as for Round 1.

Round 2

Round 3: Overlap 3 hearts (close to a semi-circle). When dry, trim approximately one-third from centre as shown, then finish as for round 1.

Round 4: Overlap 3 hearts, as for round 3. When dry, roll into a cone, bend tips out slightly, then trim approximately one-third off pointed end.

Round 3

To assemble

Glue rounds one inside the other, starting with round 1 and working in.

Round 4

SEALING

If you are making jewellery, Christmas decorations, a mobile or some free-standing item that needs to be extra strong, it will have to be sealed. There are many sealing products available on the market, for example, varnish (I use gloss finish), ceramic sealers, craft sealers, and even clear nail varnish. Be careful, as varnish tends to brown white papers, and nail varnish can blister some metallic papers, so it's a good idea to try a small sample first. Otherwise, the sealer you choose is really only a matter of preference. Always allow your finished item to dry for at least twenty-four hours before sealing.

Instructions

Liquid: Thread a piece of cotton through your finished piece, and dip into sealer until completely submerged. Lift out, and drain well. If necessary, blot on newspaper to get rid of as much excess sealer as possible. Hang to dry.

Spray: Place finished item on a clean surface, and spray well from all sides. This may need to be done in a few steps, allowing one side to dry before doing the next. Again, hang to dry.

Nail varnish: Of course, this comes with its own brush applicator. To make sure you get into all surfaces, you may have to do this in two steps, allowing one side to dry before doing the other.

CRIMPING

Crimping paper gives the same effect as crimping hair—small waves. Crimped paper can be used for bows, water, frills, etc. A commercial crimper is available, but you could try to make one yourself, using a pair of cogged wheels from a children's construction set perhaps.

METALLIC PAPERS

Metallic papers are not double sided, but are backed with white. This presents a problem for most normal shapes.

There are two ways to overcome this, both involving using the paper double:

1. Use two strips of the required length, back to back. For example, to make a 15 cm metallic gold teardrop, take two strips of 15 cm metallic gold, lay them back to back (i.e. white sides together). Apply a small amount of glue to one end and allow to dry—roll from this end. When you have finished rolling, the strip of paper that was to the inside of the roll will be longer than the outer one; trim ends to match, allow roll to loosen, glue off both ends, then pinch into shape.

2. Use a strip that is twice the length you need. Bring loose ends together, but do not crease at halfway point. Glue loose ends, and allow to dry. Roll from glued end, and a natural crease will form when you reach the other end (this means no waste).

Note: Metallic papers do not hold the roll as well as other papers, so be careful not to let them unroll too much.

MEASUREMENT CONVERSION

For ease of reference, conversions from Metric to Imperial measurements appear at the foot of each page

15mm: $^1/_{16}$"; 3mm: $^1/_8$"; 6mm: $^1/_4$"; 9mm: $^3/_8$"; 12mm: 1"; 15mm: $^3/_8$"; 20mm: $^3/_4$"; 25mm: 1"; 30mm: 1$^1/_4$"; 40mm: 1$^5/_8$"

FOR THE BEGINNER

Quilling is a very simple craft. Before you start trying to make specific shapes, take a few minutes to simply practice rolling paper onto your tool.

To roll: Lay one end of your strip along the index finger of your left hand (left handers reverse). Slide the slit in the tool over the end of the strip. Roll tool toward you. Once you have completed a few revolutions, the paper will be anchored, and you can move your index finger out of the way if you want to. Try to keep the paper straight, and roll to the end of the strip. Push the roll off the end of the tool (if you pull it, you run the risk of pulling the centre out). When you let go of the roll, it will uncurl a little.

Trouble shooting: Don't worry if your first few rolls barely uncurl at all—that just means that in your efforts to concentrate and get your roll even and straight, you have pulled on the strip as you rolled it. Relax and let the paper feed itself onto the tool; you will soon find your rolls uncurling nicely. The looser your hold on the paper, the looser and larger the finished roll will be.

ASSEMBLING THE DESIGNS

Quilled shapes are glued using white PVA glue. This glue is best as it dries clear, and does not dry so quickly as to make small mistakes impossible to correct. Tip a small amount of glue onto a tray (e.g. plastic lid from butter or margarine container or similar), and follow these five steps.

1. Roughly position pieces on card to make sure they fit as you want them to (e.g. petals around a flower look best if evenly spaced).
2. Use tweezers (fine point tweezers are best) to pick up each piece in turn (one point of tweezers goes into middle of roll, the other to outside).
3. Dip base of piece in glue.
4. Blot off excess glue on a clean part of your glue tray.
5. Reposition piece in the design.

In the following section this method will be referred to as the 'tweezer method'.

SET OF GIFT TAGS

Anne Redman

If you are new to the craft of quilling, here is a place to start. This series of gift tag designs will give you a chance to practise the basic shapes before venturing into more involved designs. The instructions for these designs are given in far more detail than the instructions in the rest of the book. Refer to previous section for details of tweezer method for assembling quilled pieces onto card. All instructions refer to lengths of 3 mm paper unless specified otherwise.

BUD FLOWERS (tight rolls and thin stems)

Instructions

Buds: 7.5 cm tight rolls
Long stem: make 2 burgundy, 2 dark pink, 2 light pink, 1 white
Medium stem: make 2 dark pink, 2 light pink, 1 white
Bud stem: make 1 light pink
Stems: Use long bladed scissors to trim very narrow strips from 6 or 9 mm green

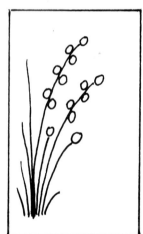

To assemble

✳ Use toothpick to 'paint' the back of stem strips with glue. Use tweezers to lift and position on card. As these pieces are so thin, and by now damp with glue, they will bend to shape quite easily.
✳ Position buds using the tweezer method. Buds are placed in pairs, one either side of stem, starting with the darkest colour, and working to white at tip.

TEARDROP FLOWER WITH SCROLLS (teardrop, leaf and V-scroll)

Special materials

3 seed pearls

Instructions

Flower (make 6): 7.5 cm cornflower blue teardrops
Buds (make 2): 7.5 cm cornflower blue teardrops
Calyx (make 2): 3 cm green V-scroll
Stems
Top: 3.5 cm green
Bottom: 2.5 cm green
Leaves (make 3): 7.5 cm green teardrops

To assemble

❋ Position flower petals at top left of card. When you are happy with the way they fit, use the tweezer method to glue in place. Add a pearl on top for flower centre.

❋ Holding stem piece in right hand, lay across left index finger. Place left thumbnail lightly on top of paper, gently pull paper out over nail. This will curve the stem. Pick up stem piece with tweezers, dip one edge in glue, blot off excess, and position with one end tucked between the petals of the flower. Repeat for other stem.

❋ Use toothpick to apply a little glue to inside of each V-scroll, add a bud. Use tweezer method to position buds and leaves. Attach a seed pearl at the end of each bud.

Option: Instead of pearls, add 3 cm bright yellow tight rolls.

SUNFLOWERS (eyes and looped leaves)

Instructions

Orange flower:
Petals (make 10): 7.5 cm eyes
Centre: 10 cm black loose roll
Looped leaves: 10 cm, 15 cm, 20 cm, 15 cm, 10 cm lime green
Stem: 7 cm lime green
Yellow flower:
Petals (make 8): 7.5 cm eyes
Centre: 7.5 cm black loose roll

Looped leaves:
7.5 cm, 10 cm, 6 cm lime green
Stem: 4.5 cm lime green

To assemble

❋ Use tweezer method to position centre of orange flower.

❋ Place petals around centre evenly (remember that you will want the stem to go directly down between two petals at the bottom of the flower). When you are satisfied that they fit well, use tweezer method to attach in place.

❋ Lift stem piece and dip one edge in glue, blot excess then position with top end between two petals.

❋ Repeat the same process with the looped leaves (in size order listed in instructions, from left to right).

❋ Repeat the above steps to assemble the yellow flower.

❋ If this seems a bit too much to start with, do just one flower.

FLOWER POT (hearts and 3 mm stems)

Special materials

3 seed pearls

Instructions

Flowers *(make 1 each in cream, lemon and bright yellow):*
Petals (make 4): 7.5 cm hearts
Stems (cut 3): from lime green, length will depend on exact siting of flowers
'Leaves': ranging in length from 3.5–7 cm, some in lime, others in emerald green, trimming top 1 cm to angle as shown
Flower pot: 30 mm x 40 mm light apricot, cut in *given shape*, score and fold forward along dotted line.
Peg: 10 cm green tight roll (not visible on finished card)

OPPOSITE: *Beginners' tags (pages 17–21)*

1.5mm: ¹/₁₆"; 3mm: ¹/₈"; 6mm: ¹/₄"; 9mm: ³/₈"; 12mm: 1"; 15mm: ³/₈"; 20mm: ³/₄"; 25mm: 1"; 30mm: 1¹/₄"; 40mm: 1⁵/₈"

To assemble

✳ Use tweezer method to attach peg about 3.5 cm up from bottom of card. Use toothpick to apply glue to bottom and sides of pot shape, and position top edge over the peg. The peg will hold the top open so stem ends can be hidden inside.

✳ Position flowers, then use tweezer method to secure in place.

✳ Cut stems to fit from each flower to inside top of pot (these can be curved as in Teardrop Flower design above, so make them a little longer than required distance). Using tweezers to hold stem, drag bottom edge through glue, blot then position on card, placing top end of each between two petals of a flower, and bottom edge into pot.

✳ Curve 'leaves' by same method as stems. Vary colours and position between flowers, again tucking bottom ends into pot. Glue using the same method as for stems.

✳ Finally, glue pearls on top of flowers where petals meet in middle.

BLUEBELLS (bells and looped leaves)

Instructions

Bluebells (make 6): 15 cm blue bell-shape

Looped leaves: 1 each 15 cm, 10 cm and 7.5 cm emerald green

Stems: emerald green, approximately 4 cm, 3 cm and 2.5 cm, glued on edge

Butterfly:
Upper wings (make 2): 7.5 cm yellow teardrops
Lower wings (make 2): 7.5 cm bright blue teardrops
Antennae: 3 cm black V-scroll

To assemble

✳ Attach leaves in desc-ending size from left to right, using tweezer method.

✳ Hold stem piece with tweezers and drag one edge through glue, blot off excess and position with bottom end between leaves. The two longer stems go between large and middle sized leaves; the smaller stem goes between middle sized and smallest leaves (refer to diagram for placements).

✳ Lift each bell with tweezers, dip one side in glue, blot off excess, position along stems.

✳ Position butterfly on card. When you are happy with the placement, use tweezer method to attach wings, then antennae.

DUCKS (petals and teardrops)

Instructions

Mother duck:
Head: 15 cm yellow teardrop
Body: 30 cm yellow petal
Ducklings (make 2):
Head: 7.5 cm yellow teardrop
Body: 15 cm yellow petal
Reeds
Reed heads (make 4): 2 cm x 6 mm dark brown tight rolls
Reed stems: use long bladed scissors to cut thin strips from 6 mm or 9 mm lime green
Water: bright blue crimped, glued on edge

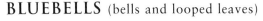

To assemble

✳ Use toothpick to paint glue onto the back of stem strips. Use tweezers to lift and position on card. Use different lengths for variety, and overlap some stems at base if preferred. Use tweezer method to attach reed heads.

✳ Position ducks on card. When you are happy with the arrangement, use tweezer method to attach.

✳ Crimp a length of bright blue, and cut pieces to fit between ducks. Use tweezer method to attach in place. Add two or three more small pieces as shown in diagram. If you are not able to crimp, you can just draw in the water with a blue marker.

15mm: ¹/₁₆”; 3mm: ¹/₈”; 6mm: ¹/₄”; 9mm: ³/₈”; 12mm: 1”; 15mm: ³/₈”; 20mm: ³/₄”; 25mm: 1”; 30mm: 1¹/₄”; 40mm: 1⁵/₈”

CHRISTMAS TAGS

POINSETTIA (leaf and tight rolls)

Instructions

Flowers

Petals (make 10): 10 cm red leaf shape
Centre (make 3): 5 cm yellow tight rolls
Leaves (make 4): 10 cm emerald green leaf shape

To assemble

✻ Position flower in top left corner of card. When you are happy with the shape, attach four or five petals using tweezer method. Using same method, attach centres, then remaining petals, and finally leaves.

This makes a great Christmas tag, but it can be done in other colours for other times of the year.

CHRISTMAS BELLS (bells and scrolls)

Instructions

Bells:

Large: join 4 cm metallic gold to 30 cm burgundy and allow to dry; roll into a bell from burgundy end to give the bell a gold rim
Small (make 2): 15 cm burgundy
Hammer (make 1): 5 cm gold tight roll
Scrolls (make 2): 7.5 cm green
Leaves (cut 3): cut folded holly leaves in emerald green

To assemble

✻ Position leaves in top left corner of card, then use tweezer method to attach in place (remember to glue on fold only).

✻ Use tweezer method to glue hammer inside large bell, then lift complete bell, dip one side in glue, blot and position as per diagram with tip just over bottom tips of leaves.
✻ Attach smaller bells in the same way.
✻ Use tweezer method to attach scrolls, noting that ends go between small and large bells.

CANDLES (cut folded leaves and tight rolls)

Instructions

Large candle: 5 cm x 40 mm white
Small candle: 5 cm x 25 mm white
Flames (make 2): 7.5 cm yellow teardrops
Berries (make 5 red, 4 yellow): 7.5 cm tight roll
Leaves (cut 10): cut folded holly leaves in emerald green

To assemble

✻ Use toothpick to apply glue down join on large candle, attach to card. Repeat with small candle. Use tweezer method to attach flames.
✻ Use tweezer method to attach leaves and berries in preferred positions, remembering to glue leaves on fold only, and placing some berries directly on the card, some on top of the leaves.

POT OF FLOWERS

Anne Redman

If you have worked through the set of gift tags, you are ready to venture on to a card. The following design uses the same basic flowers to make a full-sized arrangement.

Special materials

3 seed pearls

Instructions

Teardrop flower (make 2):
Petals (make 5): 7.5 cm white teardrops
Centre: 5 cm bright yellow tight roll
Leaves (make 2): 7.5 cm emerald green teardrops
Eye flower (make 2):
Petals (make 5): 7.5 cm pink eye

Centre: seed pearl
Leaves (make 2): 7.5 cm emerald green eyes

Heart flower (make 1):
Petals (make 4): 7.5 cm burgundy heart
Centre: seed pearl

Tight roll flowers:
Large (make 7): 7.5 cm mauve tight rolls
Small (make 5): 7.5 cm mauve tight rolls

Bluebells (make 4): 15 cm pale blue bells
Stems: varying lengths of emerald green glued on edge

Pot:
Bowl: Join 2 x 30 cm fawn strips and allow to dry. Wind as loosely as possible into a loose roll. Pinch into a fairly tall semi-circle, and push in on sides.
Handles (make 2): 6 cm fawn S-scrolls, scrolled more at the bottom end

Bee:
Head: 7.5 cm black tight roll
Body: 7.5 cm yellow teardrop
Wing: 7.5 cm white teardrop

To assemble

✳ Position pot at bottom of card. As this is such a large loose piece, it may be easier to apply glue to the card, then sit pot on top OR use toothpick or an old art brush to apply glue to back of vase, invert and attach to card. Add handles.

✳ Position teardrop, eye and heart flowers on card. When you are happy with the arrangement, glue into place.

✳ Add pearl centres on top of teardrop and heart flowers.

✳ Add stems to all the above flowers; cut a length of emerald green, use tweezers to apply glue to one edge, then position on card. Add stems for tight roll flowers and bluebells.

✳ Position tight rolls and bluebells along the stems and glue in place.

✳ Attach leaves and bee. Use fine felt tip pen to draw feelers on the bee.

✳ Add a few emerald green scrolls (4–7 cm), wherever they will fit.

Option: If you find it a little difficult to get the pot big enough, replace it with the terracotta pot from the gift tag on page 18.

OPPOSITE: For the beginner: Pot of Flowers (page 22), Easy floral designs: Lattice Roses, Jessica's Basket, Birthday Roses (pages 24–25)

15mm: ¹/₁₆"; 3mm: ¹/₈"; 6mm: ¹/₄"; 9mm: ³/₈"; 12mm: 1"; 15mm: ³/₈"; 20mm: ³/₄"; 25mm: 1"; 30mm: 1¹/₄"; 40mm: 1⁵/₈"

EASY FLORAL DESIGNS

LATTICE ROSES

Christine Meston

Card preparation

Using a tri-fold card with large rectangular cut-out, lightly pencil mark the opening onto the backing piece. Open out to work on this piece as follows:

❊ Using a ruler, lightly pencil mark a line from the top right to bottom left corners. Rule a series of lines 2 cm apart either side of this line until the rectangle is covered.

❊ Repeat, but going from top left to bottom right.

❊ Using strips of 3 mm brown, cover the first set of lines, attaching with a dot of glue at each end only.

❊ Repeat with second set of lines, but this time weave the strips in and out of the previous ones.

Note: This can also be done on a plain card, just trim ends of strips flush with edges of card.

Instructions

Folded roses:
Large (make 4): 20 cm x 6 mm pink
Medium (make 6): 10 cm x 6 mm pink
Small (make 5): 6 cm x 3 mm pink
Leaves (cut 40–50): cut folded leaves

To assemble

❊ Attach some leaves to sides of roses, attach roses to card. Add remaining leaves under edge of roses.

Option: Add a few spirals or scrolls for vines and tendrils.

JESSICA'S BASKET

Liz Dicks

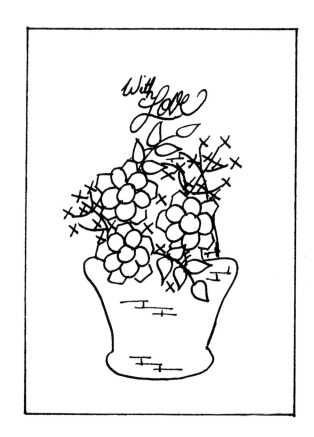

15mm: $^1/_{16}$"; 3mm: $^1/_8$"; 6mm: $^1/_4$"; 9mm: $^3/_8$"; 12mm: 1"; 15mm: $^3/_8$"; 20mm: $^3/_4$"; 25mm: 1"; 30mm: $1^1/_4$"; 40mm: $1^5/_8$"

Instructions

Basket: From 3 mm metallic gold paper, cut 23 x 10 cm strips and 24 x 7.5 cm strips. Lay the 10 cm pieces (gold side down) on a quilling board or piece of paper, and lightly tape or glue down the left end of each. Lay the 7.5 cm pieces (gold side down) above these strips and again lightly attach the top ends. Weave panel and secure all loose ends. Cut basket and handle from the patterns from lightweight card. Apply a light coat of glue to one side of each, invert and press firmly onto woven panel, placing handle diagonally. Lift completed panel, trim around shapes.

Curled roses (make 3): using red papers (see page 15)
Baby's breath (make 24): 3.75 cm x 3 mm white fringed flowers (8 per 30 cm length)
Leaves (cut 10): cut folded leaves using 9 mm dark green
Stems: cut from 1.5 mm dark green, glued on its edge

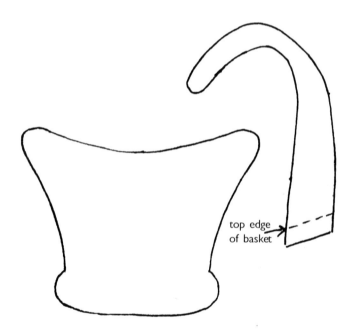

top edge of basket

To assemble

✷ Glue basket and handle to card, add roses.
✷ Attach stems, baby's breath, then leaves.

BIRTHDAY ROSES

Audrey Sheffield

Special materials

heart cut-out card
piece of silver foil paper
3 mm satin ribbon bow to match
heart punch and glitter glue (or see option below)

Instructions

Roses:
Large (make 2): 15 cm x 6 mm dusty pink
Medium (make 2): 10 cm x 6 mm dusty pink
Small (make 2): 6 cm x 3 mm dusty pink
Leaves (make 2): emerald green fringed leaves
Bluebirds (make 3): fold 1 cm bright blue in half and curve ends slightly
Stems: cut various lengths from 1.5 mm apple green
C-scroll: 7.5 cm apple green, scrolled very lightly
'Curls': cut strips of 1.5 mm apple green and pale blue in half lengthwise, scrolling and/or spiralling into curls

To assemble

✷ Attach silver paper behind heart cut-out then glue down backing piece of card.
✷ Position roses as shown.
✷ Choose a point near bottom left of heart for stems to meet. Position stems flat on card, then add leaves. Add C-scroll and curls. Attach ribbon bow over join in stems.
✷ Attach blue birds.
✷ Punch out 5 pale pink heart shapes and decorate each with glitter glue. Attach to card.
✷ Write or stamp greeting on bottom right corner.

Options:
1. Replace heart punches with 4 cm x 3 mm heart scrolls.
2. Instead of using a heart cut-out card, cut heart shape from silver paper and glue it to a plain card.

Happy Birthday!

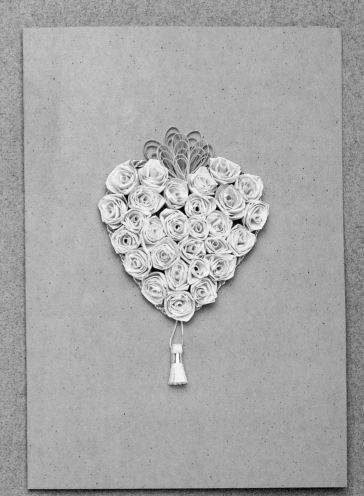

Happy Birthday
to My
Mother

LAVENDER

Jill Garsia

Special materials

mauve satin ribbon, approx. 20 cm x 5 mm, tied in a bow

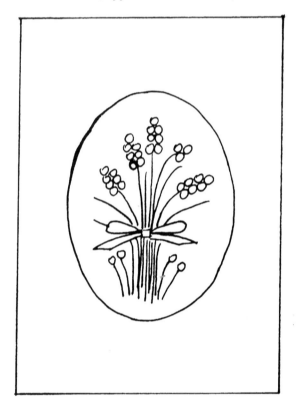

Instructions

Buds (make 35): 5 cm mauve tight rolls
Stems: cut from 1.5 mm olive green in varying lengths (some stems have no buds at all)

To assemble

✳ Position stems on edge. Add 7 buds for full flowers, 3 for small flower, and 1 for single buds.
✳ Add bow on top of stems.

Note: This design can be worked on either an oval cut-out card, or on a standard bi-fold card with an oval shape attached to the front.

HEART OF ROSES

Licia Politis

Special materials

18 cm narrow twisted gold cording

OPPOSITE: *Easy floral designs: Lavender, Heart of Roses (page 27), Happy Birthday Mum, Wild Iris (page 28)*

Fill with roses

Instructions

Folded roses (make 28): 15 cm x 6 mm cream; some will need to be slightly smaller to fit in, so don't let them all uncurl to the same size
Tassel:
Bottom: 10 cm x 9 mm cream fringed, wind into tight roll
Top: 7 cm x 3 mm cream tight roll
Binding: 1 cm x 3 mm gold
Leaves:
Bottom layer (make 4): 10 cm x 1.5 mm mid green loop as shown
Middle layer (make 3): as above using light green
Top layer (make 1): 6 cm x 1.5 mm pastel green loop as above, but forming only two loops

To assemble

✳ Lightly mark heart shape onto card and glue cording over this shape.
✳ Position roses inside heart.
✳ Join tassel top and bottom as shown and wrap gold binding around join. Cut 2–3 cm x 1.5 mm cream in half lengthwise, thread one piece through tight roll. Glue loose ends under gold cording to allow tassel to dangle freely.
✳ Position leaves at top of heart in three layers.

tassel

binding

HAPPY BIRTHDAY MUM

Clare Waterworth

Special materials

plain white card and white heart cut-out
gold dimensional paint
red satin ribbon, approximately 20 cm, tied into a bow

Instructions

Folded roses (using red paper):
Large (make 4): 15 cm x 6 mm
Buds (make 3): 7.5 cm x 6 mm
Leaves (using 7.5 cm emerald green):
(make 3): teardrops
(make approx 28): leaf shapes
Stems:
Small stems: emerald green glued on edge
Bottom stem: 3.5 cm dark green cut 3 times lengthwise to within a few millimetres of the top, so giving 4 thin stems

To assemble

✻ Glue heart cut-out onto card and paint around edge with gold paint.
✻ Position roses and buds, then stems and leaves as per diagram.
✻ Glue bow at base of heart.
✻ Tuck top end of bottom stem under bow and fan out fine stems; glue into place.

WILD IRIS (*Dietes iridaceae*)

Norma Genn

Special materials

blank card with oval cut-out
light green paper glued behind oval

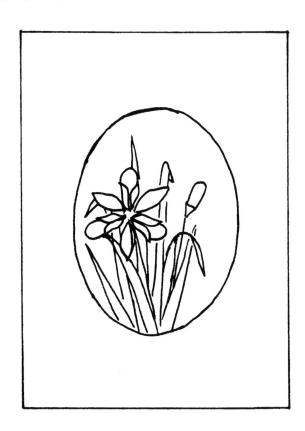

Instructions

Flower:
Centre: 20 cm x 1.5 mm apple green shallow dimensional roll
White petals (make 3): 20 cm white eyes
Two-tone petals (make 3): cut 7 cm yellow and 20 cm white; laying yellow on top of white, with one pair of ends together, glue lightly; roll from glued end; pinch into teardrop
Lavender petals (make 6): 10 cm x 1.5 mm leaf shapes; joined in pairs to make 3 petals
Bud: 13 cm white loose roll, pinch to shape
Calyx: 5 cm eucalypt green triangle
Stems: cut from 1.5 mm eucalypt green
Leaves: varied lengths cut from 9 mm olive green, approximately 4 mm wide at base, tapering to a point at the tip

To assemble

✻ Glue leaves in place on card. Fold over tips of a few to give dimension.
✻ Position flower centre; surround alternately with white and two-toned petals. Add lavender petals on top of two-toned petals, gluing at centre only, so tips sit up a little.
✻ Join bud pieces and glue in place.

15mm: ¹/₁₆"; 3mm: ¹/₈"; 6mm: ¹/₄"; 9mm: ³/₈"; 12mm: 1"; 15mm: ³/₈"; 20mm: ³/₄"; 25mm: 1"; 30mm: 1¹/₄"; 40mm: 1⁵/₈"

BUSH IRIS (*Patersonia sericea*)

Meg Prance

Instructions

Flowers (all three are the same; make 1 in each size):
Petals (make 6): long thin mauve semi-circles, joined in pairs along flat edge to make 3 petals, and twisted slightly to add variety and shape; small 10 cm, medium 15 cm, large 30 cm
Bract: 7.5 cm dark purple teardrop
Centres (make 3): gold tight rolls; small 2 cm, medium 3 cm, large 5 cm
Buds (make 9): sage green in variety of sizes (5–15 cm) and shapes (petal, semi-circle, leaf); see diagram and photograph for inspiration
Stems: 3 mm sage green
Leaves: cut in a variety of lengths, some from 3 mm sage green, and a few in 3 mm dark purple; cut tips at an angle

To assemble

✳ The flowers can be assembled on your quilling board first, if you prefer.
✳ Join the 3 petals in a triangle, position on card with one petal upright at top.
✳ Position bract opposite this, between other two petals.
✳ Attach centres on top of flower, but not touching each other.
✳ Add stems to each flower.
✳ Glue a variety of leaves around flowers, then scatter buds in a pleasing pattern.

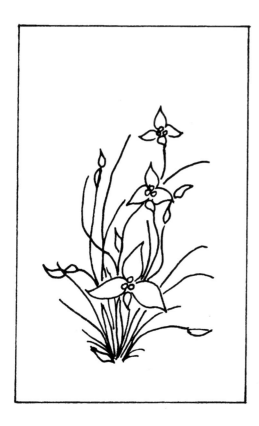

TOPIARY TREE

Jessie Beacom and Eleanor Georpalidis
My combination of the variations sent by our two designers.

Special materials

narrow satin ribbon in toning colour, approximately 20 cm, tied into a bow

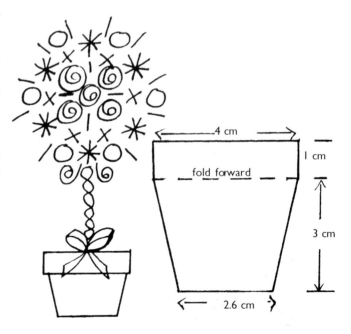

Instructions

Colours for flowers are not specified; if you wish to achieve a more elegant look, use tones of one colour, but they could be made in any combination.
Folded roses:
(make 5): 15 cm x 9 mm
(make 6): 10 cm x 6 mm
Fringed flowers (add 5 cm x 3 mm centres to some):
(make 6): 15 cm x 9 mm
(make 6): 10 cm x 6 mm.
Leaves (make approx. 18): 7.5 cm green eyes
Stem: 3 x 10 cm brown, plaited; trim if necessary
Pot: cut following pattern, from light orange paper
Scrolls (make 2): 5 cm green

To assemble

✳ Lightly mark a 6 cm diameter circle on card. Attach stem. Apply glue to side and bottom edges of pot and attach over end of stem.
✳ Attach one large rose upright in centre of circle, and remaining 4 large roses on a slight angle around it.
✳ Attach small roses around edge of circle at 1, 3, 5, 7, 9 and 11 o'clock positions.
✳ Attach large fringed flowers around edge of circle at 2, 4, 6, 8, 10 and 12 o'clock positions.
✳ Attach small fringed flowers inside circle between roses. Add leaves as preferred.

Patersonia serica
...Bush Iris...

Best
Wishes

❋ To finish, add scrolls either side of stem at base of flower ball, and 3 mm satin ribbon bow where trunk meets tub.

THE FLOWER-WATCHER

Anne Redman

Special materials

4 seed pearls

Instructions

Flowers (make 6): 15 cm dark apricot petal
Buds (make 3): 15 cm pale apricot teardrop
Leaves (make 5): 15 cm apple green petal
Bird:
Head: 15 cm Wedgwood blue teardrop
Upper body: 15 cm Wedgwood blue semi-circle
Lower body: 15 cm dark apricot semi-circle
Tail: 7.5 cm Wedgwood blue double scroll
Flower stems (make 2): 7.5 cm apple green scroll (forms one side of calyx for bud)
Bird: 15 cm double scroll—top piece forms one side of calyx for bud, bottom piece is scrolled almost back to fold
Calyxes (make 3): 3 cm apple green scroll
Scrolls (make 8): using 7.5 cm apple green (scroll some more than others)

To assemble

❋ Position flower, with a pearl as its centre. Add stems, then buds, scrolls and leaves.
❋ Join upper and lower body pieces for bird along flat edges, position bird. Add stem, bud, scroll and leaf.
❋ Add a pearl at the tip of each bud.

Options:
1. The design as given can be moved so that the bird is in any corner of the card; place the flowers in the diagonally opposite corner.
2. To convert for smaller card or tag, halve all measurements, or use bird element of design by itself.

3-D FUCHSIA

Wendy Verity

Instructions

Flower (make 3):
Calyx: 5 cm bottle green bell
Outer petals (cut 4): approx. 1 cm long from red paper
Middle petals (punch 5): circle punches from 9 mm crimson; two or three of these may need their sides trimmed into an 'ice cream' shape for a neat fit when assembled
Inner petals (punch 3): circle punches using 9 mm crimson
Stamen: 1.5 mm wide powder pink scrolls; make 4 x 1.5 cm and 1 x 2 cm
Leaves (make 5): 5 cm bottle green teardrops
Stems: 3 mm bottle green glued on edge

To assemble

❋ Attach stems to card, add one calyx at end of each stem. Add third calyx one-third of the way up the long stem.
❋ Glue one outer petal flat on card at each calyx, with the top point just touching the open end of the bell shape. Curl remaining outer petals slightly, and attach evenly around inside calyx.
❋ Place middle petals evenly inside flower, overlapping as you go.

OPPOSITE: *Easy floral designs: Bush Iris, Topiary Tree, (page 29), The Flower-Watcher (page 31)*

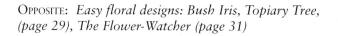

1cm: ³/₈"; 2cm: ³/₄"; 2.5cm: 1"; 3 cm: 1¹/₄"; 3.5cm: 1⅛"; 4cm: 1⅝"; 5cm: 2"; 7.5cm: 3"; 10cm: 4"; 15cm: 6"; 20 cm: 8"; 30cm: 12"; 45cm: 8"; 60cm: 24"   31

- ✤ Pinch inner petals on one side, and glue on pinch inside middle petals.
- ✤ Attach stamens to inner petals, with the longer one in the middle.
- ✤ Attach leaves.

FUCHSIAS

Anne Redman

Special materials

5 double ended stamens

Instructions

Calyx (make 3): 5 cm dark green oval
Bud:
Outer (make 2): 15 cm burgundy teardrop
Centre: 7.5 cm pink teardrop
Opening bloom:
Outer (make 2): 15 cm burgundy crescent
Middle (make 2): 15 cm pink teardrop
Centre: 7.5 cm pink teardrop
Top: 7.5 cm burgundy teardrop
Full bloom:
Outer (make 2): 15 cm burgundy eyes
Middle (make 2): 15 cm pink teardrops
Centre: 7.5 cm pink teardrop, pinched lightly to triangle shape
Leaves (make 8): 15 cm dark green leaf shape
Stems: dark green, glued on edge

To assemble

- ✤ Position calyx, outer and middle petals for all flowers.
- ✤ Cut stamens into two, varying lengths. Position two stamens in middle of bud, and four each in the other flowers. Add centre petals over stamen ends.
- ✤ Cut stems to fit, and attach in place. Add leaves.

A BLUSH OF PINK

Maureen Bowden

Instructions

Fringed flowers:
Large: use 30 cm x 15 mm dusty pink; this is not a pre-cut width ✱
Medium (make 3): 30 cm x 9 mm blush pink ✗
Folded roses:
Large (1 blush pink, 2 dusty pink): using 10 cm x 6 mm ⑥ ⑧
Small (2 blush pink, 1 dusty pink): using 7.5 cm x 3 mm ○ ⑩
Heart punch roses (make 2): in blush pink ♡
Buds (make 1 blush pink, 2 dusty pink): as 4th round of rose, and add pearl for centre ▽ ⑱
Leaves (make 1 blush pink, 10 dusty pink): 7.5 cm leaf shape
Half flower:
Petals (make 5): 7.5 cm dusty pink leaf shapes
Centre: 5 cm dusty pink tight roll

OPPOSITE: *Easy floral designs: 3-D Fuchsia (page 31), Fuchsias, A Blush of Pink (page 32), Heart and Flowers (page 34)*

15mm: ¹/₁₆"; 3mm: ¹/₈"; 6mm: ¹/₄"; 9mm: ³/₈"; 12mm: 1"; 15mm: ³/₈"; 20mm: ³/₄"; 25mm: 1"; 30mm: 1¹/₄"; 40mm: 1⁵/₈"

To assemble

❋ Position fringed flowers, then roses, buds, and finally half flower and leaves.

❋ Using gold dimensional paint, add a dot to centre of fringed flowers and heart punch roses, a line around some top edges of other roses and buds, and 2–3 dots scattered around the design.

Options: Change colour scheme; mauve and lilac, deep and light pink, aqua shades, apricot and soft peach are good combinations. To convert to a wedding card, use all cream papers on cream card, and add pearls to centre of flowers.

HEART AND FLOWERS

Tricia Fossey

Special materials

approx. 9 cm x 9 cm each satin fabric, lace fabric and thin wadding
8 cream seed pearls
white card with heart cut-out

Instructions

Flowers (make 3 dark apricot, 2 apricot):
Petals (make 4): 7.5 cm teardrops
Buds:
Petals (make 1 apricot, 2 dark apricot): 7.5 cm teardrop
Calyx (make 3): 2 cm emerald green V-scroll
S-scrolls:
Large (make 3): 7.5 cm emerald green
Small (make 3 emerald green, 2 apricot): 4 cm
Leaves (make 4): 7.5 cm emerald green teardrops
Tight rolls (make 3 apricot, 4 dark apricot): 7.5 cm

Card preparation

Trace heart shape onto backing piece. Cut wadding approximately 3 mm smaller all round than this heart, glue to card with craft glue.

Run a line of glue just outside pencil line. Cover wadding with satin fabric, stretch and press firmly into place. Trim any excess.

Repeat the above step to cover satin with lace fabric. Glue card backing piece to card front.

To assemble

❋ Following diagram for layout, position quilled pieces as follows:
Top of heart:
❋ Centre: dark apricot flower
❋ Sides (working out to edges): small green S-scroll, small apricot S-scroll, dark apricot tight roll, apricot tight roll
Bottom of heart:
❋ Centre: dark apricot flower and small green S-scroll
❋ Left (working out to edge): apricot flower, large S-scroll with leaf and apricot tight roll, apricot bud
❋ Right (working out to edge): apricot flower with dark apricot tight roll, dark apricot flower, large S-scroll with dark apricot tight roll and 2 leaves, dark apricot bud
❋ Lower right: large S-scroll with leaf, dark apricot bud

Options: This would make a lovely wedding card; work in bridesmaid's colours, or all white/cream.

IKEBANA BOWL

Moya Burns
These next three designs were inspired by a book on *ikebana*, the delightful art of Japanese floral arrangement.

Instructions

Bowl: 30 cm each in dusty pink and dusty burgundy; lay one on top of the other, roll and pinch into a semi-circle
Fringed flowers (make 5): fringe 15 cm x 6 mm yellow, join to 4 cm x 3 mm green, roll from green end ✘
Leaves:
Large leaves (cut 4): fringed leaves cut from 9 mm dark green
Looped leaves (make 2): 1 x 11 cm and 1 x 5 cm using medium green
Curved leaves (make 2 in varying lengths):
Main stem: 5 cm light green; trim end to point and pull over thumb nail to curl slightly
'Leaves' (cut 5): shorter pieces of light green, trim ends, and curl as for main stem

15mm: ¹/₁₆”; 3mm: ¹/₈”; 6mm: ¹/₄”; 9mm: ³/₈”; 12mm: 1”; 15mm: ³/₈”; 20mm: ³/₄”; 25mm: 1”; 30mm: 1¹/₄”; 40mm: 1⁵/₈”

To assemble

❊ Position bowl and flowers.
❊ Add stem for curved leaves; add 'leaves' one at a time.
❊ Finally attach looped leaves and fringed leaves.

IKEBANA IN RECTANGULAR VASE

Moya Burns

Instructions

Vase: cut from cardboard following pattern and cover with foil paper
Fringed flowers (make 4 orange, 5 yellow):
10 cm x 6 mm

Leaves (cut 12): cut folded leaves using 6 mm olive green
Stems: olive green, trim ends to point
Left: 6 cm, 6 cm, 4 cm
Right: 5.5 cm, 4 cm, 3.5 cm

To assemble

❊ Position vase. Add fringed flowers, position stems, and lastly add leaves.

IKEBANA ROSES

Moya Burns

Instructions

Any type of rose would do for this design; spiral roses were used here.

Vase: weave a 3 cm x 4 cm (approximately) panel of 3 mm strips in two tones; cut out vase shape following pattern and edge with light coloured 1.5 mm paper
Spiral roses (make 2): Cut in wavy pattern from a 4.5 cm diameter circle of white paper, (see page 14)

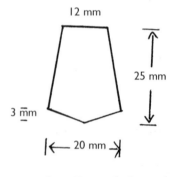

Leaves (cut 4): fringed leaves cut from 9 mm dark green
Stems: 8 cm, 4.5 cm, 3.5 cm, 2 x 2.5 cm, alternately dark and light green, trim to point and curve slightly

To assemble

❊ Attach vase, then bottom rose and leaf to its left.
❊ Position longest two stems, then add top rose and leaf.
❊ Working round to right, add stems and leaves in turn

ABOVE: *Easy floral designs: Three ikebana cards
(pages 34–35)*

OPPOSITE: *Wildflowers of the World: 'A' for Acacia
(page 38), Wattle Wishes, Native Violets (page 39)*

Best
Wishes

Acacia Beckleri
(Cootamundra Wattle)

AUSTRALIAN WILDFLOWERS

Meg Prance

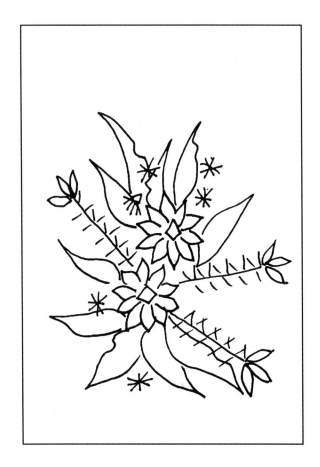

Instructions

Flannel flowers (make 2):

Petals (cut 10): fold 9 mm white in half lengthwise and cut 2 cm long petals in given shape. Unfold and bend petals slightly so tips will curve out and down.

Centre: 10 cm x 9 mm eucalypt green fringed flower

Assemble petals in a circle, one overlapping the next. You should be left with a small hole in the centre—position fringed centre to cover this.

Bottlebrush (make 3):

Flowers (make 15): 2 cm x 9 mm crimson fringed flowers

'Nuts' (make 15): bell using 5 cm x 1.5 mm eucalypt green

Stem: 5 cm light tan folded in half lengthwise to make a tented shape

Leaves (cut 3): cut folded leaves 2.5–3 cm long, using 6 mm eucalypt green

To assemble, glue each flower inside a nut. Glue five nuts along each side of the stem (approx 7 mm apart), using a ruler or pencil to support them while glue dries.

Glue last five nuts on top of stem, in between the first two sets and pointing straight up, noting that the last nut goes at very tip of stem. When completely dry, fan out fringing.

Gum blossoms (pale pink fringed flowers):

Large (make 5): 15 cm x 9 mm
Small (make 1): 5 cm x 9 mm

Gumnuts:

Large (make 5): 20 cm light tan bell
Small (make 1): 10 cm light tan bell

Leaves: using wide bottle green paper, cut 10 gum leaves varying in length from 3.5 to 5 cm. Score vein down centre and fold along scoreline to give dimension.

Attach flower inside nut, allow to dry; fan out fringing.

To assemble

✳ Position flannel flowers on card, then bottlebrush. Add leaves under top of bottlebrush.

✳ Position gum leaves, then blossoms, with tips of nuts positioned under leaves.

Option: Flannel flower petals can be tipped with light green paint. Gum blossoms can be tipped with white paint.

'A' FOR ACACIA

Licia Politis

Instructions

Letter:

Frame: fold 20 cm pastel green in half, scroll out a small amount at each end

Crossbar: 8 cm pastel green S-scroll
Leaves (make 10 pastel, 10 eucalypt green and 4 olive):
fringed leaves
Flowers (make 6 sprays of 7–8 flowers each): 3 cm x
1.5 mm wide bright yellow tight rolls

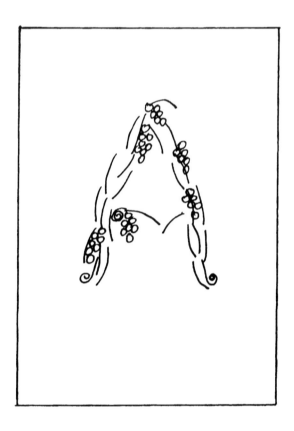

To assemble

✳ Position the letter in the centre of the card.
✳ Starting at the top, arrange leaves pointing down, some on either side, others curling over the top of the letter. Spread different colours throughout. When finished, all you should be able to see of the letter are the scrolls at the bottom and crossbar.
✳ Join flowers into sprays by gluing flowers to each other where they touch. Attach sprays on top of leaves, or cascading from underneath them, in a variety of patterns to give a dangling effect.

WATTLE WISHES

Liz Dicks

Instructions

Flowers (make 41): 15 cm golden yellow tight rolls
Leaves (cut 5 each): 1.5 mm eucalypt green x
2 cm, 1.5 cm, 1 cm, each folded in half as
shown in the diagram

To assemble

✳ Cut a piece of eucalypt green approximately 11 cm x 1.5 mm, and position on its edge, curving from top right to bottom left across card.
✳ Stems to flowers are 1–1.5 cm, to leaves 2.5–3 cm. Cut stems and attach to central stem.
✳ Attach flower sprays and leaves as shown, noting that leaves lie across top of stem.

NATIVE VIOLETS

Anne Redman
There are many species of violets found throughout the world; this pattern could be adapted for most varieties. You may need to vary the colour, or the shape of the leaves. Variations are also given for bottom petal.

Instructions

Flowers (make 3):
Upper petals (make 4): 7.5 cm mauve teardrops
Lower petal: (make 2): 10 cm mauve teardrops OR
    (make 1): 20 cm mauve heart OR
    (make 1): 20 cm mauve teardrop, pinched at point only; push back rounded end to make shape short and squat rather than long and thin
Centre (make 2): 5 cm x 1.5 mm yellow tight roll
Buds (make 4):
Flower: 7.5 cm mauve teardrop
Sepal: 3 cm eucalypt green V-scroll

Large leaves (make 3): 2 x 30 cm eucalypt green crescents, pinched tighter on one end
Medium leaves (make 2): 2 x 15 cm eucalypt green crescents, pinched tighter on one end
Small leaves (make 12): 7.5 cm eucalypt green teardrops
Stems: cut from eucalypt green, glued on edge

of black. If you roll your papers toward yourself, place black on top of brown. This will ensure that the brown runs out before the black, giving a black outer edge.)
Outer 'leaves' (cut 9): 1 cm long, using petal pattern and bottle green paper; use blade of scissors or tweezers to press a line along centre, then roll tips out
Middle petals (make 17): as for outer leaves, but using yellow paper.
Inner petals (make 17): cut as for outer leaves; press fold only halfway, place a dot of glue in fold, allow to dry and snip the tip off glued end
Stems: cut from 1.5 mm bottle green, cutting ends at angle; glue on edge
Leaves (cut 4): using bottle green paper, follow pattern; score along centre line, and curve tips (score in veins as well, if you like)

To assemble

✳ To assemble double leaves, glue two crescents together along flat edge (pin onto quilling board until dry). When dry, pinch top end again.

✳ Attach large leaves at bottom of card. Position flowers and buds and when you are happy with the arrangement, attach to card. They can be free assembled on the quilling board first, if you prefer.

✳ Attach slightly curved stems to flowers and buds, with lower ends positioned between leaves.

✳ Add small leaves in pairs along stems.

✳ Add medium leaves on top of large ones, covering spaces between leaves, and stem ends.

SCULPTURED SUNFLOWER

Wendy Verity

Instructions

Flower (make 3):

Centre: use yellow pencil or pastel to mark a stripe along one edge of 30 cm brown; fringe this strip (along yellow edge), and a 30 cm black strip. Lay strips on top of each other, with yellow edge facing black, roll together. (If you roll your papers away from yourself, place brown on top

To assemble

Assemble flowers and their stems one at a time, so petals of one overlap another if needed. Start with top flower, then flower on left, and lastly bottom right:

✳ Attach centre of flower to card, then space outer leaves evenly around it.

✳ Attach middle petals around centre, over the top of the outer leaves, but allowing the leaves to show through.

✳ Attach the inner petals around centre, trying to offset positions so that lower layers show through.

OPPOSITE: *Wildflowers of the world: Sculptured Sunflower (page 40), Red Clover, Spider Lily (page 42); Forget-me-not (page 43)*

Red Clover

- ❊ When all flowers are finished, attach stems and short stems for leaves (5–10 mm). Finally add leaves.

RED CLOVER

Meg Prance

Option: Make the paper for the leaves shiny by coating well with PVA glue and allowing to dry.

Instructions

Large flower (make 20): 5 cm x 1.5 mm rose pink teardrops, twist 6 into petal shapes

Large sepals (cut 3): shiny green cut folded leaves approx. 1 cm long

Small flower (make 10): 5 cm x 1.5 mm rose pink teardrops, twist 2 into petal shapes

Small sepals (cut 3): shiny green cut folded leaves approx. 7 mm long

Large leaves (make 3): cut from shiny green paper, approx. 2 cm long; score centre line and veins, curve edges back slightly

Medium leaves (make 3): cut from shiny green paper, approx 1.5 cm long; score centre line and veins, pinch together at base, add a dot of glue to hold

Small leaves (cut 3): cut folded leaves using shiny green paper, approx.1 cm long

Stems: cut from 1.5 mm sage green, and glue on edge

To assemble

- ❊ Arrange large flower with pinched end of all pieces pointing up. Apply glue to base only of each quilled piece, and allow each row to overlap about half the one above.
  Top row: 4 teardrops
  Row 2: 1 petal, 3 teardrops, 1 petal
  Row 3: 1 petal, 2 teardrops, 1 petal
- ❊ When first three rows are in place, add sepals so that last two rows will overlap them.
  Row 4: 1 petal, 3 teardrops, 1 petal
  Row 5: 2 teardrops
- ❊ Arrange small flower in the same way:
  Top row: 2 teardrops
  Row 2: 3 teardrops
  Row 3: 2 teardrops
- ❊ When first three rows are in place, add sepals so that last row will overlap them.
  Row 4: 1 petal, 1 teardrop, 1 petal
- ❊ Attach stems in place, then leaves.

SPIDER LILY

Anne Redman

Instructions

Flowers (make 2):

Petals (make 3): 2 x 15 cm purple crescent (pinch bottom end only lightly)

Centre: 2 cm x 6 mm yellow fringed flower 

Buds (make 5): 10 cm eucalypt green eyes 

15mm: 1/16"; 3mm: 1/8"; 6mm: 1/4"; 9mm: 3/8"; 12mm: 1"; 15mm: 3/8"; 20mm: 3/4"; 25mm: 1"; 30mm: 1 1/4"; 40mm: 1 5/8"

Leaves (cut 4): eucalypt green in long, thin triangle shape, tapering to a pointed end

To assemble

✤ To assemble petals, glue flat edge of crescents together (pin to quilling board until dry). Assemble flowers on quilling board.

✤ Position upper flower, then buds at its base (following diagram). Add stem and leaves.

✤ Attach top flower resting across buds and stem as shown.

position of buds

FORGET-ME-NOT

Anne Redman

Instructions

Full flowers (make 3):
Petals (make 5): 7.5 cm Wedgwood blue teardrops
Centre: join 4 cm x 1.5 mm yellow to 5.5 cm x 1.5 mm white; roll from yellow end into tight roll
Part flowers (make 2):
Central petal: 7.5 cm Wedgwood blue teardrop
Side petals (make 2): 7.5 cm Wedgwood blue petal
Sepal: 7.5 cm lime green heart, pushed flat
Buds (make 6): 7.5 cm lime green teardrops
Spent flowers (make 2): 10 cm lime green tulips
Stems: lime green, glued on edge
Leaves (cut 4): 3.5–5 cm long lime green, cut to shape given; score in veins, curve top over, and pinch at centre of base

To assemble

✤ Free assemble full flowers on quilling board, placing centre on top of finished flower.

✤ Position main stem, then add two full flowers flat onto card, to right of stem in positions shown, and four buds at top end of stem.

✤ Attach short stems to two buds, part flowers and spent flowers, position following diagram.

✤ Add last full flower with one side resting on top of main stem.

✤ Apply glue at fold on leaves, attach middle two, then outer two

SCOTCH THISTLE

Wendy Verity

Instructions

Large flower
Top: join 30 cm x 9 mm fringed mauve to 3 cm x 9 mm fringed dark green. Roll onto tool from  mauve end, with fringes facing toward tool handle. Leaving 'flower' on tool, glue loose end and apply glue to end of roll, allow to dry. Join 30 cm x 3 mm dark green at join on flower, allow to dry. Roll into very gradual cone shape, extending away from fringed centre (see diagram). Glue loose end, smear glue around inside on cone shape, dry, then remove.
Bottom: 60 cm dark green rolled into gradual cone shape as for top.
When finished, these two pieces should fit together to form a ball, with a flower at the top. If the bottom half is not quite the same size as the top, add a small piece of green, and wind on a few more rounds.
Small flower (make 2) Follow method for large thistle, but using the following lengths:
Top: 10 cm x 9 mm fringed mauve, 3 cm x 9 mm fringed green, 15 cm x 3 mm green
Bottom: 30 cm x 3 mm green
Stems: cut a length of 3 mm dark green. Cut triangles along one side, giving a jagged effect, to within 2–2.5 cm of top.
Leaves (cut 3): 4 cm x 9 mm cut folded leaves, shape as given.

Flower stems (make 12): 1.5 mm wide mid-brown cut in small lengths; curve slightly

Leaves (cut 5): using shiny green paper, approx 1.3–1.5 cm wide, cut folded leaves in varying lengths from 4 cm–9 cm; curve tips over on two or three

To assemble

✻ Join two pieces of each thistle together to form a ball. Cut 3 cm x 3 mm green and roll around centre to hide join.

✻ Attach thistles to card, then stems and leaves.

BLUEBELLS

Meg Prance

Option: Make the paper for the leaves shiny by coating well with PVA glue and allowing to dry.

Instructions

Flowers (make 8): cut 2.5 cm x 6 mm purple and trim one edge into 5 points as shown. Attach to one end of 30 cm x 3 mm purple, roll into bell shape from 3 mm end. To give a realistic shape, roll straight for 5 or 6 turns; then gradually into a dimensional roll for half the strip; then wider for the remainder. Apply glue inside bell and allow to dry. Fold back 6 mm points

Buds (make 2 in each size): using purple papers. Apply glue inside finished bells, and allow to dry. Attach smaller bottom bell inside top one.

Large:
Top: 15 cm dimensional roll/bell
Bottom: 10 cm dimensional roll/bell

Small:
Top: 12 cm dimensional roll/bell
Bottom: 7.5 cm dimensional roll/bell

Slivers (make 12): cut slivers of purple approx 1 cm long, 1 for each flower and bud

Main stems (make 2): 1 x 10.5 cm and 1 x 9 cm in 1.5 mm mid-brown, curve slightly and glue on edge

To assemble

✻ Position main stems on card.

✻ Attach a flower stem into top of each flower and bud. Arrange as shown along lower side of main stems, placing 1 large and 1 small bud at the top of each.

✻ Attach slivers adjacent to flower stems, but on opposite side of main stems as shown, and add leaves.

BUTTERCUP

Meg Prance

Option: Make the paper for the petals shiny by coating well with PVA glue and allowing to dry.

Instructions

Flower petals (cut 10): using the shiny yellow paper, cut in shape given (or punch using a balloon punch), then trim end. Gently curve into slight cup shape over finger or tool to give dimension.

Centre for large flower: fringe 5 cm each sage green and yellow, place one on top of the other, and roll into tight roll with the yellow to the outside. Add 5 cm x 6 mm fringed yellow and continue rolling. When dry, fan out 6 mm yellow only.

Opposite: *Wildflowers of the world: Scotch Thistle, (page 43) Bluebells, Buttercup (page 44), Waratah (page 46)*

15mm: ¹/₁₆"; 3mm: ¹/₈"; 6mm: ¹/₄"; 9mm: ³/₈"; 12mm: 1"; 15mm: ³/₈"; 20mm: ³/₄"; 25mm: 1"; 30mm: 1¹/₄"; 40mm: 1⁵/₈"

Sepals for smaller flower (cut 3): from lime green paper, approx 1 cm long and 2 mm wide, in given shape.
Flower stems: approx 7.5 cm and 6.5 cm x 1.5 mm sage green, glued on edge.
Tiny leaves (cut 10): using lime green paper, 5–7 mm long, and 1–2 mm wide
Leaves (make approx 30): 7.5 cm–30 cm lime green eyes, flattened completely. The arrangement of the leaves can vary as you prefer, but those illustrated are arranged as follows (in each case, working from bottom left side of stem and around in a clockwise direction, in three sets):
Left leaf: 7.5 cm, 10 cm, 15 cm, 15 cm, 15 cm, 10 cm, 7.5 cm
15 cm, 7.5 cm, 20 cm, 7.5 cm, 15 cm
7.5 cm, 15 cm, 7.5 cm, 10 cm, 7.5 cm, 7.5 cm.
Right leaf: 7.5 cm, 10 cm, 15 cm, 15 cm
15 cm, 15 cm, 30 cm, 20 cm, 20 cm
15 cm, 10 cm, 15 cm, 10 cm.
Leaf stems (make 2): 6–7 cm lime green, fold in half and glue together (3–3.5 cm finished).

To assemble

✳ Assemble five petals, shiny side up, into large flower. Slightly overlap each petal, and glue only at base. Note that bottom petal overlaps on both sides. Add centre.
✳ Assemble remaining five petals for smaller flower, with shiny side out. Overlap a little more than for previous flower, and arrange into cup shape. Add sepals, allow to dry, then bend right back.
✳ Add stems to flowers, and tiny leaves in groups of four as per diagram.
✳ Position leaves—these can be fully or partially assembled on your quilling board first if you prefer. Attach to card and add stems.

WARATAH

Lynne Mayes

Special materials

12 cm x 10 cm toning paper
oval cut-out card

Instructions

Waratah (using red paper):
Central petals (make 15): 10 cm loose rolls; pinch into 11 teardrops, 3 crescents, 1 eye
Scrolls (make 6): 5 cm
Outer petals: cut from candle paper
Leaves (cut 5): in dark green; score veins using stylus or other blunt instrument
Gum blossoms:
Fringed flowers (make 2): 10 cm x 6 mm yellow or cream ✗
Nuts (make 2): 30 cm brown
Leaves (cut 6): eucalypt green

To assemble

✳ Attach toning paper behind oval cut-out.
✳ Position waratah leaves in centre of oval.
✳ Position waratah outer petals in an arc (see diagram for placement).
✳ Assemble central petals of waratah so the bottom edge just covers the top edge of the outer petals (these can be free assembled on a quilling board first, if you prefer). Add scrolls. Curl outer petals up and over bottom edge.
✳ Position gum leaves, then flowers and nuts.

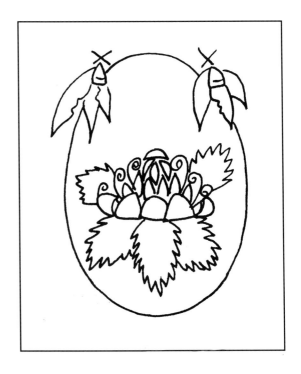

15mm: ¹/₁₆”; 3mm: ¹/₈”; 6mm: ¹/₄”; 9mm: ³/₈”; 12mm: 1”; 15mm: ³/₈”; 20mm: ³/₄”; 25mm: 1”; 30mm: 1¹/₄”; 40mm: 1⁵/₈”

ANIMALS AND BIRDS

SWAN SONG

Meg Prance

Instructions

Head: Attach 4 cm black to 40 cm white; roll from black end to join; glue, dry. Continue rolling and form a loose roll in white
Beak: 15 cm blue loose roll pinched to shape
Crest (make 2): white crescents, 1 x 7.5 cm, 1 x 5 cm
Body:
Top row (make 4): 30 cm white teardrops
Middle row (make 5): 30 cm white teardrops
Bottom row (make 4): 30 cm white teardrops
(make 1): 20 cm white teardrop
Bottom edge (make 4): 20 cm white teardrops
Neck (make 5): 20 cm white teardrops
Tail (make 2): 45 cm white crescents
Folded rose: 21 cm x 9 mm burgundy
Fringed flowers:
Small (make 1): using 5 cm x 3 mm dark pink ✗
Large (make 3): using 5 cm x 6 mm dark pink ✳
Pink flowers (make 2): ○
Petals (make 4): 7.5 cm pale pink teardrops
Leaves (make 11): 5 cm x 1.5 mm dark green teardrops

Cut leaves (make 5): blue cut folded leaves, approx 1 cm long using 9 mm paper
Water (make 12): 15 cm blue leaf shapes

To assemble

❋ Tail: position right crescent. Left crescent overlaps at left hand point only (sits on an angle, not flat on card).
❋ Body:
Top row: position one teardrop flat on card to left of tail. Add remaining 3 teardrops in an arch as shown, each slightly overlapping the previous one.
Middle row: Position one teardrop, flat on card, just under bottom of tail crescent. Add remaining teardrops, overlapping the previous one as in top row, but also slightly overlapping the points of top row teardrops.
Bottom row: Position smaller teardrop, flat on card, at the right hand edge as shown. Add large teardrops as for middle row, overlapping each other and the row above.
Bottom edge: Position one teardrop flat on card at right hand edge as shown. Add remaining teardrops with top edges resting on row above.
❋ Neck: Position teardrops as shown, add head and beak.
❋ Make a small peg to support rose—position peg and rose. Add blue leaves.
❋ Position pink flowers below rose, then fringed flowers.
❋ Scatter quilled leaves around flowers.
❋ Make ribbons and bows using crimped 3 mm burgundy. Form into loops and position ends under flowers and leaves (see photo for placement).
❋ Position leaf shapes for water.

PARROT

Glenys Thompson

Instructions

Eye: join 1 cm white to 1 cm black, roll from white end into a tight roll
Beak: 4 cm grey triangle and 5 cm grey crescent
Tail (do not use tool): loop lengths of bright blue to fit into marked area
Branch: cut from strips of dark brown

1cm: ³/₈”; 2cm: ³/₄”; 2.5cm: 1”; 3 cm: 1¹/₄”; 3.5cm: 1³/₈”; 4cm: 1⁵/₈”; 5cm: 2”; 7.5cm: 3”; 10cm: 4”; 15cm: 6”; 20 cm: 8”; 30cm: 12”; 45cm: 8”; 60cm: 24”

Leaves (make 4): 15 cm eucalypt green leaf shape
Fringed flowers (make 2): 4 cm x 6 mm yellow ✳
Parrot: use 7.5 cm lengths in specified colours to fill each section; the type of roll can be varied to suit the shape to be filled (the sample was worked using mainly teardrops)

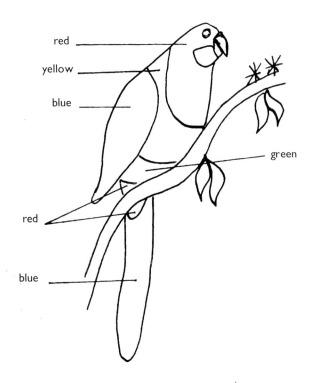

To assemble

✳ Lightly trace parrot shape onto card, and position branch and eye.
✳ Assemble quilled pieces into each section of parrot.
✳ Position leaves and flowers.

Option: The parrot could be assembled on your quilling board—trace shape onto baking paper, assemble bird, then lift and glue onto card.

ROBIN'S CHOIR

Betty Kowald

Special materials

cream paper or lightweight card, approx. 4 cm x 3 cm

Instructions

Small birds (make 3):
Head: glue 1 cm white to 10 cm black; roll from white to join, glue and dry; roll black into loose roll
Breast: 8 cm red petal
Tail: 10 cm black heart
Body (make 5–6): 5 cm black teardrops
Beak: 5 mm yellow folded in half
Large bird:
Head: as for small birds but use 1.5 cm white and 30 cm black
Upper breast: 5 cm red teardrop
Lower breast: 12 cm red teardrop
Tail (make 2): 10 cm black eyes
Beak: 5 mm yellow folded in half
Body (make 18–19): 5 cm black teardrops
Leaves (make 6): 5 cm green eyes

To assemble

✳ Cut book shape from the pattern in cream cardboard or paper, add lines and mark edges with gold pen. Draw branch onto card with brown marker pen. Attach bottom edge and left half of book to card (top right corner lifts and sits on large bird).
✳ Assemble birds and leaves as shown.

CENTIPEDE

Heather Tathem
This design looks really cute assembled on a card cut in a leaf shape from green cardboard.

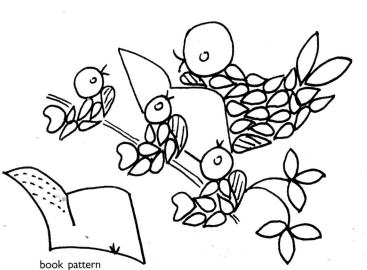

book pattern

15mm: ¹/₁₆"; 3mm: ¹/₈"; 6mm: ¹/₄"; 9mm: ³/₈"; 12mm: 1"; 15mm: ³/₈"; 20mm: ³/₄"; 25mm: 1"; 30mm: 1¹/₄"; 40mm: 1⁵/₈"

Instructions

Head: 15 cm yellow loose roll
Body (make 5): 7.5 cm loose rolls in bright colours
Legs (make 3): 7.5 cm black double scrolls
Antennae: 7.5 cm black V-scroll

LEAPING DOLPHINS

Eileen Stephenson

Instructions

Dolphins (make 2) using grey paper:
Body: 30 cm crescent
Top fin: 6 cm loose roll, lightly pinched to shape
Bottom fin: 4 cm loose roll, lightly pinched to shape
Tail: 10 cm crescent
Eye: 4 cm black tight roll
Birds (make 3): approx. 2 cm bright blue folded in half and curved to shape
Water:
Surface: crimped blue
Ripples: light blue and white crimped
Sun: 30 cm bright yellow loose roll, pinch to quarter circle
Rays: crimped bright yellow (varying lengths), glued on edge

To assemble

✳ Position dolphins, add water pieces (glued on edge), then sun and birds.

PREVIOUS PAGE: *Animal and bird cards: Swan Song (page 47), Parrot, Robin's Choir, Centipede (page 48), Leaping Dolphins, Dolphin (page 50)*

DOLPHIN

Annette Wann

Instructions

All worked in cornflower blue.
Snout:
Upper: 15 cm oval
Lower: 10 cm oval
Eye: 10 cm x 1.5 mm black tight roll
Flippers:
Upper: 15 cm oval, slightly curved
Lower: 10 cm oval, slightly curved
Tail: 30 cm loose roll, pinched to shape
Body (make 3): 7.5 cm petals
(make approx. 19): 10–15 cm teardrops

To assemble

✳ This may be easier to assemble on a quilling board. Trace shape onto paper (layer 2 of board), then finish board. Follow outline of dolphin to assemble. When dry, lift and glue onto card.
✳ Position eye and the three petals in a circle around it.
✳ Add remaining quilled pieces (if assembling straight onto card, it may be easier to lightly trace the shape onto your card first).

Option: Add water and/or birds as on the Leaping Dolphins design above.

GREEN TREE FROG

Meg Prance

Special materials

2 x 4 mm joggle eyes

Instructions

Frog
Body:
Inner (make 2): 30 cm lime green triangles (see diagram for dimension)
Middle (make 4): 15 cm bottle green eyes (long and thin)
(make 2): 15 cm bottle green crescents (long and thin)
Outer (make 4): 30 cm lime green leaf shapes
Side bumps (make 2): 7.5 cm lime green semi-circles
Nose: 7.5 cm lime green crescent
Back legs (make 2):
Upper: 30 cm lime green eyes
Lower: 30 cm bottle green eyes
Feet: 15 cm lime green triangles
Webbing: use small lengths of lime green, folded to fit
Toes (make 8): 2 cm bottle green tight rolls

15mm: ¹/₁₆”; 3mm: ¹/₈”; 6mm: ¹/₄”; 9mm: ³/₈”; 12mm: 1”; 15mm: ³/₈”; 20mm: ³/₄”; 25mm: 1”; 30mm: 1¹/₄”; 40mm: 1⁵/₈”

Instructions

Body: 30 cm grey loose roll
Head: 15 cm grey loose roll
Ears (make 2): 7.5 cm black petal
Muzzle: join 3 cm black to 7.5 cm white and allow to dry; roll from black end to join, glue and dry; finish winding, and let white uncoil into a loose roll; push into oval shape
Feet (make 2): 7.5 cm black triangle
Tail: 3-4 cm black, trim one end to a point
Ball: 30 cm red loose roll
Grass: looped leaves in emerald green, from left to right: 14 cm, 9 cm, 7 cm, 7 cm, 9 cm

To assemble

✳ Assemble dog, noting that muzzle sits on top of face. Add joggle eyes.
✳ Curve tail, and glue into place, then add grass and ball.
✳ Use fine point black marker pen to draw in tufts of hair on dog's head and movement marks at tip of tail.

CAT GIFT TAG

Marilyn Sullivan

Special materials

Approx. 20 cm toning 5 mm satin ribbon tied in a bow

Instructions

Use the colours you prefer.
Body: 30 cm loose roll
Head: 15 cm loose roll, pinched to make ears
Tail: 7.5 cm scroll

To assemble

✳ Position quilled pieces as shown, attach bow at neck, and draw in whiskers.

Front legs (make 2):
Legs (make 2): 15 cm bottle green triangles
Feet: 7.5 cm lime green loose rolls
Webbing: as for back legs
Toes (make 10): 2 cm bottle green tight rolls
Dragonfly (worked in 1.5 mm papers):
Head (make 1): 5 cm light green tight roll
(make 2): 2 cm light green tight rolls
Body:
Upper (make 2): 4 cm light green tight rolls
Lower (make 3): 3 cm light green tight rolls, slightly flattened
Wings:
Top (make 2): 6 cm pale mauve teardrops
Bottom (make 2): 5 cm celery green or cream teardrops

To assemble

✳ Attach frog body pieces, working from centre out (you may need to adjust pinching on some pieces slightly to get a good fit).
✳ Add legs, then feet, webbing and toes.
✳ Position joggle eyes.
✳ Assemble dragonfly in bottom right corner of card.

DOG

Anne Redman

Special materials

2 x 3 mm joggle eyes
red satin ribbon for bow, 3 mm wide

DREAMTIME LIZARD

Meg Prance

Special materials

2 x 6 mm joggle eyes

Instructions

Body:
(make approx 35): 7.5 cm dark brown loose rolls, pinched into teardrops, semi-circles or eyes as necessary to fit into pattern
(make approx 20): 3 cm triangles in earthy tones (orange, yellow, bone, etc.)
Head:
(make 1): 30 cm dark brown loose roll, pinched lightly to form snout
(make 3): 1.5 cm bone tight rolls
Legs (make 4):
Upper: 7.5 cm dark brown teardrop
Lower: 2 cm dark brown, folded in half, glue at loose ends only
Feet (make 4): 2 cm dark brown, folded in half, glued together
Toes (make 4): 2 cm dark brown tight rolls

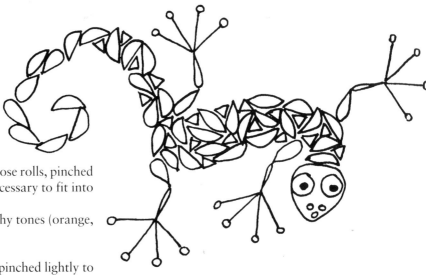

To assemble

✳ Assemble body pieces following the diagram and photograph, varying colour of triangles throughout.
✳ Add legs and feet.
✳ Position head, noting that bone tight rolls sit between the coils of the loose roll. Add joggle eyes.

Animal and bird cards: Green Tree Frog (page 50), Dog, Cat Gift Tag (page 51), Dreamtime Lizard (page 52)

<small>Opposite: *Wedding and anniversary cards: Silver Anniversary, With this Ring (page 54); Wedding Flowers and Doves (page 55); Heart of Roses, Congratulations (page 56)*</small>

15mm: ¹/₁₆"; 3mm: ¹/₈"; 6mm: ¹/₄"; 9mm: ³/₈"; 12mm: 1"; 15mm: ³/₈"; 20mm: ³/₄"; 25mm: 1"; 30mm: 1¹/₄"; 40mm: 1⁵/₈"

SILVER ANNIVERSARY

Ellen McCartney-Lees

Instructions

Folded roses (make 20): Cut 20 cm lengths of 6 mm burgundy and lightly glue 3 mm silver along top edge; when dry, fold and roll roses
Fringed flowers (make 12): 10 cm x 9 mm silver ✗
Leaves (cut 15): cut folded leaves using 9 mm silver

To assemble

❋ Lightly pencil the number 25 onto the card, write or stamp wording.
❋ Position roses and fringed flowers as shown. Add leaves in and around flowers.

WITH THIS RING

Rosa Robartson

Special materials

5 cm x 7 mm white satin ribbon
hologram wrapping paper (optional)
small piece of white card

Instructions

Bible: Draw shape onto white card following outline diagram. Colour in page edges with gold pen. Make a small slit in this area; insert ribbon, gluing end down at back and cutting free end at an angle
Pegs (make 4): 7.5 cm white tight rolls
Candles (make 2): cut approx. 10 cm x 7–8 mm from hologram paper and roll into taper (dimensional roll)
Flames (make 2): 3 mm x 4 cm of the same paper or 7.5 cm x 1.5 mm lemon teardrop
OR
Candles (make 2): 5 cm x 40 mm white/metallic gold/silver
Flames (make 2): 7.5 cm lemon teardrops
Daisies:
Large (make 4): join 15 cm x 6 mm fringed white to 15 cm x 3 mm cream, roll from 3 mm end
Small (make 3): 15 cm x 6 mm fringed flower ✗
Folded roses:
Large (make 2): 15 cm x 6 mm white
Small (make 1): 10 cm x 6 mm white
Leaves (cut 8 in 9 mm, 6 in 6 mm): pastel green fringed leaves 2–2.5 cm long
Rings (make 2): cut 2 small pieces of 1.5 mm metallic gold, place them back to back, and join at one end. Roll around a pen (or similar), trim ends to match and glue, leaving until completely dry. Make one ring slightly larger than the other

15mm: $^1/_{16}$”; 3mm: $^1/_8$”; 6mm: $^1/_4$”; 9mm: $^3/_8$”; 12mm: 1”; 15mm: $^3/_8$”; 20mm: $^3/_4$”; 25mm: 1”; 30mm: $1^1/_4$”; 40mm: $1^5/_8$”

Other leaves:
(make 7): 10 cm emerald green leaf shape
(make 7): 10 cm apple green leaf shape
Top scrolls (make 2 each): 5 cm and 3 cm emerald green
Bottom scroll: 12 cm emerald green C-scroll
Birds (make one each in pinks and blues):
Body: 15 cm pale teardrop
Head: 7.5 cm dark teardrop
Wing: 10 cm dark teardrop
Tail: 3 cm dark V-scroll and 2 cm scroll
Rings (make 2): fold 6 cm metallic gold in half, roll around handle of tool, trim ends to match and glue; leave on tool until completely dry
Heart: cut 2 x 4 cm metallic gold, place back to back and fold in half, placing a dot of glue at the fold to hold; roll into a heart scroll, trim ends to match and add dot of glue where tops meet

To assemble

✤ Attach pegs to back of Bible, position on card.
✤ Attach candles with bottom edges tucked under Bible, then add flames.
✤ Arrange flowers, roses, then leaves as shown.
✤ Attach one ring on top of Bible, then second ring slightly overlapping the first.

WEDDING FLOWERS AND DOVES

Anne Redman
Worked in pastel colours, this is a lovely anniversary card. To convert to a wedding card, work all the flowers in white, and the leaves in dark olive and eucalypt greens.

Special materials

seed pearls

Instructions

Curled rose: cream paper (see page 15)
Fringed flowers (make 3): 15 cm x 6 mm cream
Buds (make 4 each):
7.5 cm fawn teardrop
7.5 cm cream teardrop
7.5 cm pale apricot teardrop
Top leaves:
(make 2): 15 cm emerald green leaf shape
(make 2): 15 cm apple green leaf shape

To assemble

✤ Stamp greeting. Position rose and fringed flowers, then scrolls. Add heart in middle of bottom scroll.
✤ To make ribbon, fold 6 cm cream in half. Attach to card, tucking fold under lower edge of rose. Place rings at ends of ribbon. Add leaves and buds.
✤ Assemble birds as shown, noting that wing is placed on top of the body.
✤ Add a pearl at the tip of each bud.

HEART OF ROSES

Desley Mole

Instructions

Folded roses (using ivory papers):
Large (make 8): 21 cm x 9 mm
Medium (make 8): 14 cm x 6 mm
Small (make 4): 7 cm x 3 mm
Buds (make 2): 7 cm x 9 mm
Leaves (approx 29): cut folded leaves using olive green
Bells (make 2): 90 cm metallic gold
Hammers (make 2): 7.5 cm metallic gold tight rolls

To assemble

* Lightly draw heart shape on card. Write message below.
* Starting at centre top position, attach roses in order from top to bottom of heart outline.
* Insert hammers inside bottom edge of bells. Attach bells to card.
* Position leaves in and around roses and bells.

CONGRATULATIONS

Enid Kenny

Special materials

approx. 15 cm pearl edging
4 seed pearls
white card with oval cut-out

Instructions

Bells:
(make 1): 60 cm silver
(make 2): 45 cm silver
Hammers (make 3): 5 cm silver tight roll
Ribbon loops:
(make 2): 20 cm white teardrops
(make 2): 10 cm white teardrops
Ribbon centre (make 2): 3.5 cm white tight rolls
Ribbon ends (make 4): 3 cm white scrolls
Dove:
Body: 15 cm white petal
Wing: 7.5 cm white petal
Head: 7.5 cm loose roll
Beak: 5 mm x 1.5 mm yellow folded in half
Petals (make 22-24): 7.5 cm white leaf shape
Leaves (cut 7): cut folded leaves using silver

To assemble

Quilled pieces should overlap edge of oval.
* Write or stamp the word 'Congratulations' in centre of oval, and glue down backing piece of card.
* Attach hammers to bells; add bells at bottom left of oval.
* Attach a ribbon centre, on its side, above large bell, and large teardrops either side. Add second centre on top of first, and smaller teardrops on top of larger ones. Position scrolls between bells.
* Position bird's body, head and beak, add wing on top of body. Cut a small rectangle of light grey paper for envelope and glue in place.
* Assemble full flowers using seven petals; part flowers using four or five petals. Add seed pearl for each centre.
* Scatter leaves around flowers as preferred.
* Attach pearl edging over uncovered edges of oval.

Option: Also looks great in cream and gold

OPPOSITE: *Boys' stuff: Scarecrow, Checkmate (page 58); Barbershop Quartet (page 59)*

Happy Birthday

BOYS' STUFF

SCARECROW

Anne Redman

Instructions

Scarecrow
Head: 30 cm yellow loose roll
Hat: 15 cm black loose roll pinched to shape
Body: 30 cm brown rectangle
Arms (make 2): 15 cm brown rectangles
Legs (make 2): 30 cm lime green rectangles
Feet (make 2): 10 cm yellow eye
Straw: fringe 6 cm x 9 mm and 2 cm x 6 mm yellow, trimming randomly as shown
Hair: attach 1.5 cm x 6 mm on top of 1.5 cm x 9 mm
Hands (make 2): 1.5 cm x 9 mm, folded into a concertina
Waist (make 2): 5 mm x 9 mm
Ankles (make 2): 5 mm x 9 mm
Pumpkin
Inner (make 2): 10 cm orange semi-circles
Outer (make 2): 20 cm orange crescents
Stalk: 2 cm emerald green folded as shown
Tail: 2 cm emerald green tight roll
Leaves (make 5): 10 cm emerald green tulip
Vines:
(make 3): emerald green scrolls, approx. 3 cm and 2 x 4 cm
(make 1): 10 cm emerald C-scroll
Crow
Body: 7.5 cm black loose roll
Head: 6 cm black loose roll
Wings (make 2): 5 cm black petals
Beak: 3 cm yellow triangle
Tail (make 2): 2 cm black folded in half and gently bent to shape
Flying crows (make 2): 2 cm black, folded in half and bent gently to shape.

To assemble

✳ Cut two lengths of 3 mm brown, 5 cm and 7.5 cm, for scarecrow's frame. Position top of upright approx. 4.5 cm down from top of card, and crossbar 1.5 cm down the upright.

✳ Attach hair to bottom edge of hat, waist straw to top edge of legs, and ankle straw to bottom edge of legs.

✳ Position head just above crossbar, add hat, body, arms, legs and feet. Fold straw down flat over quilled pieces. Glue straw hands in place.

✳ Cut 2.5 cm x 3 mm black and position for hat brim. Cut two small diamonds of red and attach on top of legs at knee position.

✳ Join inner pumpkin pieces, then glue outer pieces around them before positioning on card. Add stalk and tail.

✳ Position vines, and add leaves.

✳ Assemble crow on right arm, and add flying crows.

CHECKMATE

Kerry Schemioneck

Special materials

white oval cut-out card
thin black card approx. 8 cm square
4 metallic seed beads ☻

Variation: I used the king from this design to make a Thank-you card for a team manager. Working on a plain white card, I simply added three pawns:
Head: 10 cm loose roll
Neck: 4 cm C-scroll
Body: 20 cm loose roll pinched to a triangle

BARBERSHOP QUARTET

Nancy Evans

Card preparation

To make the checked background, open card out to work on backing piece. Lightly mark lines about 2 cm in from both top and bottom, and 1.5 cm in from each side. Mark a series of parallel lines 1 cm apart between these two lines. Use a Stanley knife or similar to cut along the lines.

Cut black card into 1 cm wide strips. Weave in and out of white section, making sure the ends are hidden inside when card is closed. Glue backing piece in place.

Instructions

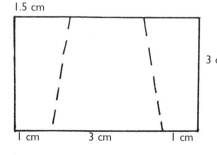

Crown:

Peaks (make 4): 7.5 cm black loose roll, pinched to a triangle
Tight rolls (make 6): using 2 cm black
Brim: 2 cm x 1.5 cm black rolled in a tight roll (2 cm long)
Face: 20 cm black crescent
Cloak: 5 cm x 3 cm black, creased as shown in diagram, and folded forward
Cloak decorations (make 2): 2 cm white S-scrolls

To assemble

* ❈ Apply glue to back of folded cloak, and centre on chequered panel.
* ❈ Add face, crown and cloak decorations.
* ❈ Attach a bead at the top of each peak on the crown.

Instructions

Singers (make 4)

Hair: 1 x 7.5 cm, 1 x 3.75 cm black petals
Eyebrows (make 2): 5 mm black curved, and glued on edge
Eyes (make 2): 2 cm black tight rolls
Moustache (3 singers use 2 cm black, 1 singer use 3 cm black): fold in half and curl ends
Mouth: 3.75 cm loose roll, squeezed into an oval shape with centre coils pushed to outside so you are left with just an oval outline
Bowtie: 1.5 cm red; nip in centre with tweezers and glue at back to hold
Shoulders: 4.5 cm x 1.5 mm black; fold in half and in reverse direction at quarters to give an M-shape
Waistcoat: lengths of 1.5 mm red placed approx. 3 mm apart; trim tops to fit the slope of the shoulders, and glue flat on card
Buttons (make 3): 1 cm x 1.5 mm black tight rolls, rolled very tight on a small needle OR use a few small black seed beads
Musical notes (make 8): 3 cm x 1.5 mm black tight roll, leaving approx. 8 mm unrolled (5 mm for stem, 3 mm for tail)

To assemble

✲ Position pieces following the diagram, and in the following order: hair, eyebrows, eyes, moustache, mouth, bowtie, shoulders, waistcoat, buttons, and lastly musical notes.

MOTORBIKE

Margery Hamer

Instructions

Tank: 45 cm red teardrop
Seat: 30 cm black loose roll, pinched to shape
Light: 30 cm shallow silver bell
Exhaust: 10 cm x 9 mm silver tight roll, laid on side
Engine: 2 x 10 cm silver, back to back, rolled and pinched into diamond
Wheels (make 2): place 2 x 30 cm silver back to back, lightly glue to join at one end. Attach 30 cm black to one strip at open end. With loose silver strip to inside, roll to join. Trim silver ends to match, then lightly glue and allow to dry. Continue rolling and form a loose roll.
Mudguards (make 2): 2.5 cm red curved slightly
Handlebars: fold 7.5 cm silver in half (silver sides out), join 4 cm black to each end and roll into double scroll (silver will only hold a curve, so you can scroll all the way)

To assemble

✲ Assemble motorbike in this order: seat and tank, engine, handlebars, then light, exhaust, wheels and mudguards.

GRANDFATHER CLOCK

Meg Prance

Instructions

Work in dark brown unless otherwise stated.
Base
Box: 45 cm loose roll pinched square plus piece of crimped paper to fit around outside of square

Sides (make 2): 7.5 cm scroll
Bottom and top (make 2): 7.5 cm C-scroll, scrolled just a little at each end
Middle
Pendulum: 75 cm x 1.5 mm tight roll (any colour); place on wrong side of gold candle paper, trace shape, cut out then glue on top of roll; attach one round of 1.5 mm gold around outside of tight roll
Hanger: approx. 3 cm x 1.5 mm metallic gold, glued flat
Weights (make 3): 2.5 cm x 25 mm gold candle paper rolled around a toothpick; fold small pieces of 1.5 mm gold (vary lengths) in half and glue in top
Sides (make 2): 7.5 cm scroll
Top: 7.5 cm C-scroll, scrolled just a little at each end
Top
Outer face: circle of white card approx. 22 mm diameter
Inner face: circle of gold candle paper approx. 12 mm diameter
Decorations (make 13): 2 cm x 1.5 mm gold tight rolls
Face surrounds: length of crimped paper to fit
Sides (make 2): 7.5 cm scrolls
Top: 45 cm semi-circle
Knob: 1 x 7.5 cm, 1 x 5 cm bells; when dry, attach smaller bell inside larger as shown and add a small piece of 1.5 mm brown in top

To assemble

This design is probably best assembled as you go, working from the bottom up.

15mm: ¹/₁₆"; 3mm: ¹/₈"; 6mm: ¹/₄"; 9mm: ³/₈"; 12mm: 1"; 15mm: ³/₈"; 20mm: ³/₄"; 25mm: 1"; 30mm: 1¹/₄"; 40mm: 1⁵/₈"

✤ Base: Position square, crimped piece, then sides; add top and bottom C-scrolls.

✤ Middle: Position side and top scrolls. Attach pendulum hanger, then pendulum. Finally add weights at slightly varying heights.

✤ Top: Position side scrolls, then top and knob. Add crimped paper, then make sure face measurement as given will fit, altering if necessary. Glue gold circle into middle of white one. Use gold pen to write numbers in Roman numerals around white circle. Cut out a pair of hands from black paper or card, and position on face. Attach face in position, then draw a circle around its outer edge with a gold pen. Add decorations around edges as shown.

Boys' stuff: Motorbike and Grandfather Clock (page 60)

CHILDREN'S CARDS

CAROUSEL WITH BABY TOYS

Marilyn Whitfield

Special materials

light blue paper approx. 6 cm square

Instructions

Carousel roof:
Scrolls (make 8): 7.5 cm light blue scrolls, scrolled only a small amount
C-scroll: 15 cm light blue, bent lightly into a semi-circle, and scrolled both ends a small amount
Fillers (make 10): 4 cm yellow tight rolls
Top: 15 cm yellow tight roll
Pole: tight roll using 5 cm x 40 mm yellow candle paper; wrap 3 mm light blue in a spiral down pole and secure ends
Bear (worked in dark brown):
Head: 7.5 cm loose roll
Body: 15 cm loose roll
Ears, arms and legs (make 6): 5 cm tight rolls
Duck (worked in yellow):
Body: 15 cm petal
Head: 7.5 cm teardrop
Ball (make 2): join 2 x 15 cm in contrasting bright colours, roll into a tight roll
Block: 15 cm loose roll, pinched square, topped with letter A cut from 1.5 mm paper
Rattle:
Handle: 3 cm x 8 mm tight roll, laid flat on card
Ball: 15 cm tight roll (use two or more colours if preferred)

Option:
1. You could add grass:
(make 4): 6 cm lime green looped leaves
(make 2): 7.5 cm lime green teardrops
(make 1): 6 cm lime green tight roll

To assemble

✳ Cut roof shape from light blue paper, glue to card. Attach C-scroll around outer edge of paper, then fill in with remaining roof pieces. Add top and pole.

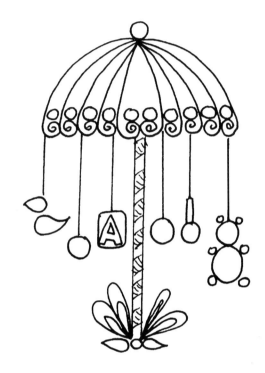

✳ Cut varying lengths of yellow and light blue 1.5 mm papers for strings, glue to card and attach toys.
✳ Add grass at foot of pole if you wish.

CLOWN

Anne Redman

Instructions

Head: 15 cm white loose roll
Hat: join 4 cm yellow to 15 cm red, roll from yellow end to join, glue and allow to dry; complete rolling and form into loose roll, pinch to triangle shape
Hair (make 2): approx. 1.5 cm x 9 mm fringed yellow
Body: 30 cm lime green loose roll
Arms (make 2): 15 cm yellow teardrops
Legs (make 2): 30 cm orange teardrops
Shoes (make 2): 7.5 cm lime green eye
Balloons (make 1 each in red, yellow and bright blue): 30 cm loose rolls

15mm: ¹/₁₆”; 3mm: ¹/₈”; 6mm: ¹/₄”; 9mm: ³/₈”; 12mm: 1”; 15mm: ³/₈”; 20mm: ³/₄”; 25mm: 1”; 30mm: 1¹/₄”; 40mm: 1⁵/₈”

To assemble

✳ Attach hair to each side of head, and hat on top of head.

✳ Position pieces following the diagram, then use black marker to draw in balloon strings.

HICKORY DICKORY DOCK

Tricia Fossey

Special materials

5 cm x 2 cm gold mesh
1 x 3 mm joggle eye
small piece cream cardboard

Instructions

Clock face border:
(make 8): 15 cm yellow leaf shape
(make 7): 7.5 cm yellow tight rolls
Centre of face: 7.5 cm yellow tight roll
Hands:
(make 1 x 6 mm, 1 x 9 mm): 7.5 cm red tight rolls
(make 2): 4 cm cream teardrops
Clock base:
(make 8): 15 cm apple green teardrops
(make 4): 7.5 cm emerald green scrolls
(make 5): 7.5 cm emerald green tight rolls
Pendulum:
30 cm emerald green tight roll
approx. 3.5 cm emerald green, glued on edge
Mouse:
Body: 15 cm grey teardrop
Ears (make 2): 7.5 cm grey teardrops
Tail: 2 cm black, taper one end to a point, then scroll
Nose: 4 cm black tight roll
Whiskers (cut 4): use thin strips of black, approximately 1 cm long
Pot: cut from dark green, edge top with 3 mm gold
Plant (using 1.5 mm papers in pastel green unless otherwise stated):
Leaves (make 1 x 15 cm, 2 x 7.5 cm): folded leaf shape
Flowers (make 5): 7.5 cm tight roll
Stem: approx 3.5 cm
Scrolls (make 2): 4 cm dark green

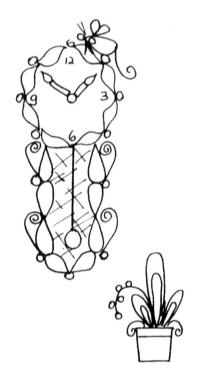

To assemble

✳ Cut 4 cm diameter circle from cream cardboard for clock face, and mark with 3, 6, 9 and 12 o'clock positions. Attach top end of gold mesh under bottom edge of circle, and attach completed piece to card.

✳ Space yellow border shapes evenly around face, add centre and hands.

✳ Position green border shapes around gold mesh below clock face as shown.

✳ Attach 4–5 mm at one end of pendulum length to tight roll. Attach opposite end within border around face, and glue tight roll on top of mesh.

✳ Position mouse at top of clock.

✳ Position plant leaves, stem and 'flowers'. Apply glue to sides and bottom of pot, and glue over ends of leaves and stem.

BIRTHDAY WISH FAIRY

Anne Redman

Special materials

1 x 3 mm joggle eye

Instructions

Fairy
Head: 15 cm flesh loose roll
Bodice: 15 cm dark aqua heart
Sleeve: 7.5 cm dark aqua oval
Hand: 4 cm flesh tight roll
Skirt (make 2 aqua, 3 dark aqua): 15 cm teardrops
Legs (make 2): 7.5 cm flesh ovals

15mm: ¹/₁₆”; 3mm: ¹/₈”; 6mm: ¹/₄”; 9mm: ³/₈”; 12mm: 1”; 15mm: ³/₈”; 20mm: ³/₄”; 25mm: 1”; 30mm: 1¹/₄”; 40mm: 1⁵/₈”

Feet (make 2): 4 cm flesh eyes

Wings (make 2): attach 15 cm yellow to the back of 15 cm metallic gold at one end only; roll into a loose roll, trim ends to match, glue, pinch to teardrop

Flower hat:

(make 3): 4 cm x 1.5 mm white teardrops

(make 1): 4 cm x 1.5 mm yellow tight roll

Wand:

Star: cut 20 cm metallic gold, bring ends together and glue without folding strip in half; roll into loose roll, and pinch into star shape

Handle: approx 2 cm dark aqua, glued on edge

Frog:

Body: 15 cm lime green teardrop

Feet: 10 cm lime green teardrop

Crown: small piece of metallic gold folded to shape

Toadstool:

Top: 30 cm red crescent

Stalk: 15 cm white teardrop

To assemble

✤ Position fairy's head, bodice, skirt, wings, legs and feet.

✤ Join hand to end of sleeve, and assemble flower hat.

✤ Position wand. Add sleeve piece to top of bodice, with hand touching handle of wand. Place hat on top of head.

✤ Attach toadstool, frog crown, and joggle eye.

✤ Add thin strips of green under toadstool for grass.

LITTLE MISS MUFFET

Anne Redman

Special materials

3 x 3 mm joggle eyes

Instructions

You will find making up this design a lot easier if you assemble the tuffet, Miss Muffet's skirt, the spider, her hat,

OPPOSITE: *Children's cards: Carousel with Baby Toys, Clown (page 62), Birthday Wish Fairy, Hickory Dickory Dock (page 63), Little Miss Muffet (page 65)*

and even her arms and hands, on your quilling board before attaching to card.

Tuffet (make 5): 15 cm x 1.5 mm dark green teardrops

Miss Muffet:

Head: 15 cm flesh loose roll

Hat: 10 cm dark mauve crescent

Brim: 10 cm dark mauve C-scroll

Hair: trim a piece of tan down to approx. 1 mm wide, wind into a spiral and cut into 3 or 4 short lengths for hair

Mouth: cut a small piece of red

Bodice (make 2): 15 cm mauve teardrops

Sleeves:

Front: 15 cm mauve semi-circle

Back: 10 cm mauve semi-circle

Hands (make 2): 4 cm flesh tight roll

Skirt:

Top (make 3): 15 cm mauve teardrops

Hem (make 4): 7.5 cm dark mauve teardrops

  (make 3): 4 cm dark mauve loose rolls

Legs:

Front: 10 cm flesh oval

Back: 15 cm flesh oval

Shoes (make 2): 7.5 cm mauve eyes

Bowl: 10 cm tan crescent

Spoon: small piece of silver folded to shape

Spider:

Body: 10 cm black loose roll

Legs (make 8): 1 cm black, fold ends as shown

To assemble

✤ Assemble tuffet (3 teardrops pointing up, 2 down), then position on card.

✤ Join hands to end of sleeves, hat crown to brim and shoes to end of legs. Attach back leg at right edge of tuffet.

✤ Assemble skirt on quilling board, and attach over tuffet and back leg.

✤ Position bodice, head, back arm and front leg, then bowl and spoon.

✤ Place front arm on top of bodice, with hand on bowl.

✤ Add hair and hat, mouth and joggle eye.

✤ Draw spider's web in top left corner of card. Assemble spider, and add two joggle eyes; attach to card. Draw thread from spider to web.

CHRISTMAS CARDS

MERRY CHRISTMAS

Chris Dicks

Special materials

3.5 x 4 cm thin black cardboard for cover of Bible
3 x 3.5 cm thin white cardboard for Bible pages
plain red card

Instructions

Candles: 1 x 6 cm, 1 x 7 cm gold, glued flat on card
Flames (make 2): 15 cm yellow teardrop
Holly:
Leaves (make 4): 10 cm emerald green diamond
Berries (make 4): 7.5 cm red tight roll
Fringed flowers: 1 x 15 cm x 9 mm white
1 x 15 cm x 9 mm lemon
Bookmark: 4.5 cm red, cut one end into V

To assemble

✳ Fold both pieces of card for Bible in half, glue together on fold. Use black pen to scribble in the impression of words. You could also mark around the edges of the 'pages' with gold pen if you like.
✳ Stamp or write greeting at top of card, and position Bible near the bottom, gluing on fold only.
✳ Add candles with bottom ends just under Bible; add flames.
✳ Position flowers and holly as shown.

CHRISTMAS GREETINGS

Trina Hawkins

Special materials

plain ivory card

Instructions

Bottlebrush (make 3): edge 30 cm x 9 mm burgundy with 1.5 mm gold, glue well and dry completely, then fringe. Roll into dimensional roll. (You will probably lose some small pieces of gold when you fringe this piece.)

15mm: ¹/₁₆"; 3mm: ¹/₈"; 6mm: ¹/₄"; 9mm: ³/₈"; 12mm: 1"; 15mm: ³/₈"; 20mm: ³/₄"; 25mm: 1"; 30mm: 1¹/₄"; 40mm: 1⁵/₈"

Large gum blossoms (make 2):
Nut: 30 cm brown bell
Flower: edge 7.5 cm x 9 mm red with 1.5 mm wide silver (as for bottlebrush), dry, fringe and roll into fringed flower
Small gum blossoms (make 6):
Nut: 15 cm brown bell
Flower: as for large flowers, but using 4 cm x 6 mm red
Wattle (make 6): 5 cm x 6 mm yellow fringed flower ✗
Flannel flowers (make 3):
Petals (cut 8): fold 25 mm white candle paper in half lengthwise (so you can cut two at a time), mark with petal shape and cut out
Centre: 5 cm x 6 mm eucalypt green fringed flower ⊗
Leaves: cut some fringed, some folded, in different shades of green

To assemble

✴ With a gold marker, rule lines 5 mm in from each edge of the card.
✴ Pencil mark a large letter C, and write the balance of greeting in gold.
✴ Position quilled flowers following the diagram, and add leaves as preferred.

SCROLL AND CANDLE

Lorraine Poltock

Special materials

4 x 11 cm paper
plain dark green card

Instructions

Candle (make 7): 6 cm red ovals
Flame: join 3.5 cm yellow to 6 cm white, dry. Roll from yellow end, pinch into teardrop
Holly:
Berries (make 3): 7.5 cm red tight rolls
Leaves (make 3): 15 cm green diamond OR cut folded leaves
Poinsettia:
Petals (make 6): 15 cm red teardrops
Centre: 15 cm yellow tight roll
Fringed leaves (make 10): 1.5–2 cm long cut from 9 mm emerald green

To assemble

✴ Following diagram and photograph for guidance, apply gold dimensional paint around edges of the rectangle of paper, and use a paint brush to spread lightly. Write or stamp greeting across centre. Scroll top right and bottom left corners, then centre on card.
✴ Attach holly leaves and berries as shown, then candle and flame.
✴ Position leaves around the candle.
✴ Free assemble poinsettia on quilling board, then position on top of leaves at base of candle as shown in the diagram.

A CHILD IS BORN

Anne Redman

Special materials

plain cream card

Instructions

Manger: Cut a thin piece of card to the shape shown in diagram. Starting at the top, cover with layers of 3 mm brown, each strip slightly overlapping the one above. Trim edges.
Legs of manger (make 2): fold 2 cm brown in half at an angle, trim ends straight
Hay: fringe 3 cm each in 6 mm and 9 mm yellow and trim to irregular shape shown in diagram
Jesus:
Head: 7.5 cm x 1.5 mm flesh loose roll
Body: 20 cm x 1.5 mm ice blue semi-circle
Halo: 5 cm x 1.5 mm metallic gold oval
Mary:
Face: 10 cm flesh teardrop

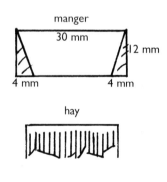

Cap: 10 cm cornflower blue crescent
Veil: 30 cm cornflower blue leaf shape
Arm: 10 cm cornflower blue teardrop
Hand: 7.5 cm flesh teardrop, loosened only slightly
Back: 30 cm cornflower blue leaf shape
Body and knees: 30 cm cornflower blue petal
Legs: 15 cm cornflower blue eye
Halo: 7.5 cm x 1.5 mm metallic gold oval
Joseph: as for Mary, but clothes are worked in mushroom
Star: lay 2 x 30 cm metallic gold strips back to back, glue lightly at one end; starting at glued end, roll onto tool, trim ends to match. Form loose roll and pinch into uneven star
Angels (make 2):
Head: 5 cm flesh loose roll
Dress: 15 cm white teardrop, pinched to shape
Sleeve: 4 cm white crescent
Hand: 4 cm flesh tight roll
Wings (make 2): using 10 cm metallic gold, bring ends together and glue without folding in half, roll from glued end, and pinch into teardrop

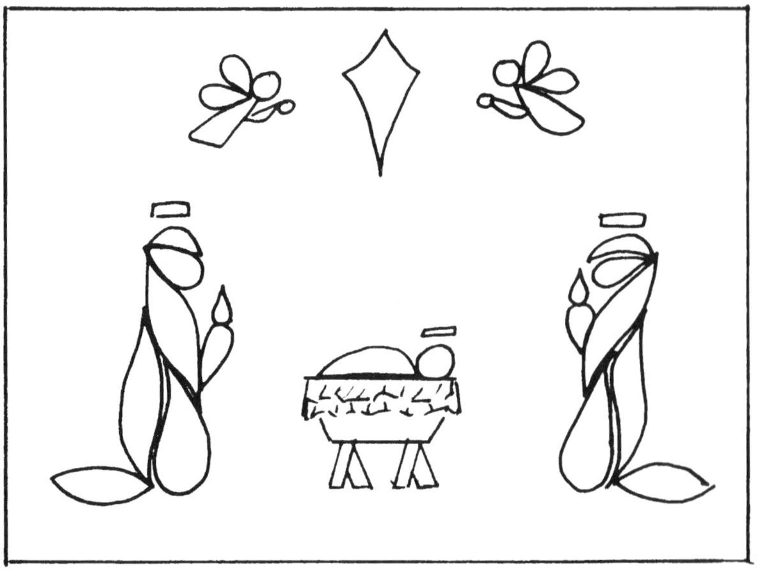

To assemble

- Attach top edge of 9 mm fringed yellow behind top edge of manger, then attach 6 mm fringed yellow on top of 9 mm. Fold both forward and down over manger.
- Position manger, manger legs, and Jesus, noting that halo is glued on its side.
- Position Mary and Joseph, then star and angels.

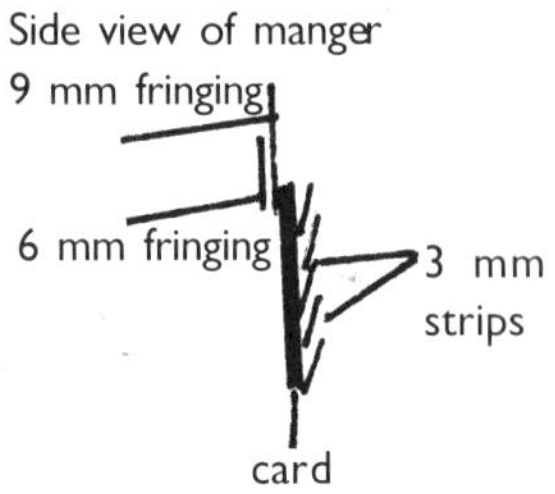

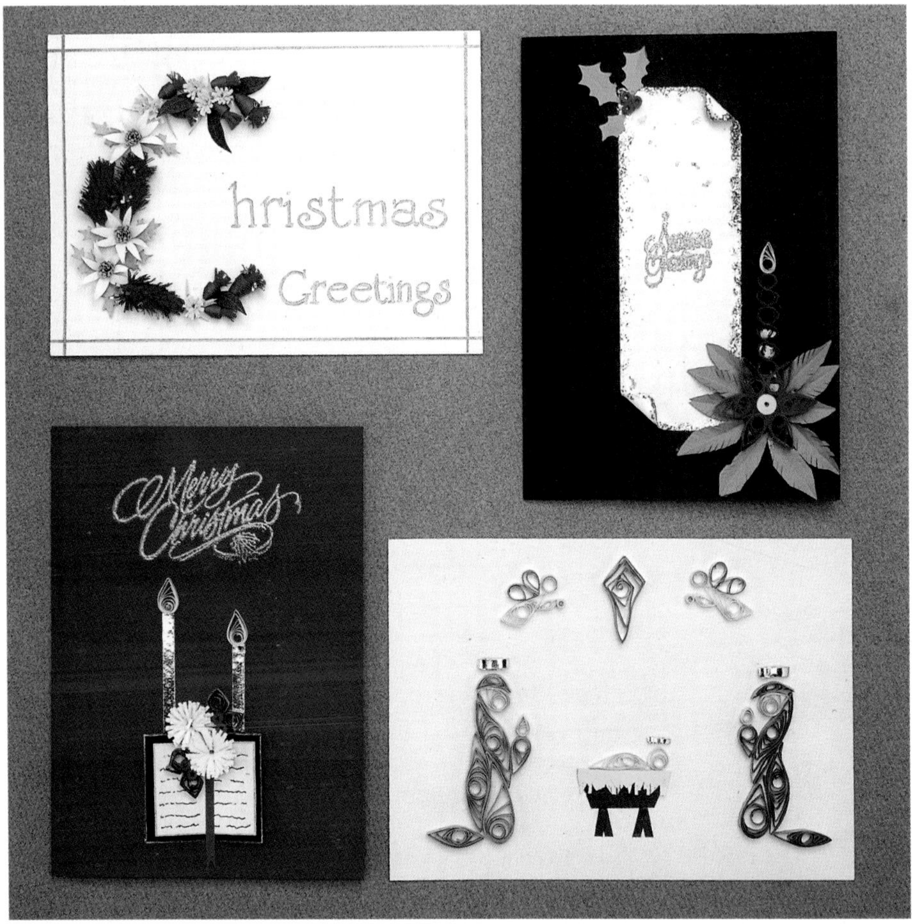

Christmas cards: Merry Christmas, Christmas Greetings (page 68), Scroll and Candle, A Child is Born (page 69)

OPPOSITE: *Angel (page 71) and Christmas tree (page 70) decorations; Wreath earrings; Poinsettia earrings (page 70)*

15mm: 1/16"; 3mm: 1/8"; 6mm: 1/4"; 9mm: 3/8"; 12mm: 1"; 15mm: 3/8"; 20mm: 3/4"; 25mm: 1"; 30mm: 1 1/4"; 40mm: 1 5/8"

SPECIAL PROJECTS

CHRISTMAS EARRINGS

Tricia Fossey

Tricia uses a neat trick to ensure her earrings look just right. She adds a length of metallic gold to each of the green strips for the wreath earrings, and to the red strips for the poinsettia earrings, glues them and allows to dry completely. When she rolls the strips she allows them to uncoil until the gold just overlaps itself. This also helps to ensure the rolls are all the same size.

Special materials

pair fish hook fittings
4 jump rings

Instructions

Wreath earrings
Wreath (make 6): join 10 cm lime green to 3 cm gold, dry, then roll from green end and pinch into leaf shape
Joiners (make 6): join 7.5 cm lime green to 1.5 cm gold, dry, then roll from green end into tight rolls
Bottom (make 2 yellow, 1 red): 7.5 cm tight rolls
Top:
(make 2): 7.5 cm x 1.5 mm red tight rolls
(make 1): 7.5 cm x 1.5 mm yellow teardrop
Candle: 5 cm x 12.5 mm gold
Flame: 7.5 cm x 1.5 mm orange teardrop

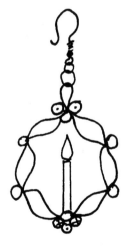

Poinsettia earrings
Petals (make 9): join 10 cm red to 3 cm gold, dry, then roll from red end and pinch into leaf shape
Centres (make 3): 7.5 cm yellow tight roll
Top (make 3): 7.5 cm red tight rolls

To assemble

❋ Earrings are most easily assembled on the quilling board.
❋ Join quilled pieces following the diagrams. Allow to dry for at least 24 hours.
❋ Seal following instructions on page 16.
❋ Join jump rings in pairs, threading fish hook fitting through top jump ring; thread the central quilled piece at the top of the earring through the lower jump ring.

Option: To convert earrings to clip-on style:
Place finished earring (before sealing) upside down on white backing side of gold candle paper, trace shape and cut out.
    Attach gold paper behind earring, and allow to dry for at least 24 hours.
    Seal following instructions on page 16.
    Use hot glue gun or similar strong glue to attach a clip fitting to each earring.

CHRISTMAS TREE DECORATION

Anne Redman

Instructions

Pot:
30 cm red loose roll, pinch to rectangle shape
3 cm yellow tight roll
Star: using 15 cm metallic gold, bring ends together and glue without creasing in middle; roll from glued end into loose roll and pinch into star
Decorations (make 20–25): 7.5 cm tight rolls in a mixture of silver, gold, red and yellow
Tree:
(make 7): 7.5 cm dark green V-scrolls
(make 7): 10 cm dark green V-scrolls
(make 3): 15 cm dark green V-scrolls
(make 1): 10 cm dark green teardrop

To assemble

❋ Work on a quilling board. Starting at the top of the tree, and using the cross and lines on the quilling board to keep your work symmetrical, position scrolls in given order. Glue where they touch, and push pins into the board to hold pieces while the glue dries:

15mm: ¹/₁₆”; 3mm: ¹/₈”; 6mm: ¹/₄”; 9mm: ³/₈”; 12mm: 1”; 15mm: ³/₈”; 20mm: ³/₄”; 25mm: 1”; 30mm: 1¹/₄”; 40mm: 1⁵/₈”

scroll number	strip length
1	7.5 cm
2	10 cm
3	10 cm
4	7.5 cm
5	7.5 cm
6	10 cm
7	15 cm
8	15 cm
9	10 cm
10	10 cm
11	15 cm
12	7.5 cm
13	7.5 cm
14	10 cm
15	7.5 cm
16	10 cm
17	7.5 cm
18	teardrop

✳ Attach star. Position red rectangle for pot, and attach yellow tight roll in its centre.

✳ Glue tight rolls on their side between scrolls, scattering colours to ensure variety.

✳ Allow to dry for at least 24 hours, then seal (see page 16).

✳ Slip a length of fine gold cord through star for hanging.

ANGEL DECORATION

Anne Redman

This design involves metallic papers formed into teardrops. As metallic paper is one-sided, for a professional finish it must be used double. See page 16 for details.

Instructions

Head: 30 cm flesh loose roll
Dress (make 9): 15 cm burgundy teardrops
Hem (make 5): 15 cm double metallic gold teardrops
Wings (make 3): 30 cm double metallic gold teardrops
Sleeves (make 2): 20 cm burgundy loose roll, pinched to shape
Hands (make 2): 10 cm flesh loose roll, pinched to shape
Candle: 5 cm x 2.5 mm gold paper
Flame: 7.5 cm yellow teardrop

To assemble

✳ Begin assembly on the quilling board.

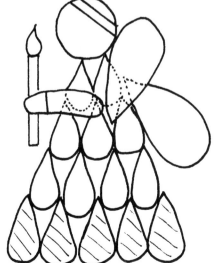

✳ Glue flame on top of candle. Insert candle between hands.

✳ Allow to dry for at least 24 hours, then seal. Thread a thin piece of gold thread through angel's head to hang.

Option: For a more interesting look, make all teardrops slightly off-centre.

GOLD TRINKET BOX

Anne Redman

This project is quite involved. You will need a quilling board to assemble the design. The teardrops can be made in the usual way, but I have made mine off-centre (see instructions page 12), giving the box a beautiful finish. All quilling is worked in white, and spray-painted gold on completion.

Special materials

oval papier-mâché box approx. 11.5 cm x 8.5 cm
lightweight cardboard approx. 12 cm x 9 cm
gold spray paint
black acrylic paint (e.g. folk art paint)
paintbrush
40 cm x 6 mm gold braid

Instructions

Box preparation

Trace around lid onto the card, then draw another oval approximately 5 mm inside the first line. Cut out smaller oval. Use Blu-Tack to secure centrally on top of lid.

Following manufacturer's instructions, apply two coats of gold paint to top of lid (edges only are gold) and to box. Allow to dry, and remove card. You may need to add a coat of varnish over the gold to protect it; I found that the paint I used tarnished with handling.

Apply two coats of black paint to top of lid, leaving a gold band approximately 3 mm wide around the edge.

When paint is quite dry, use craft glue to attach gold braid to the top of lid, covering the join between colours.

5 cm scrolls

Quilling board

Place lid on quilling board, centring carefully over central cross. Trace the shape onto baking paper. Draw another oval approximately 7 mm inside the first one (to allow for the braid). Erase outer oval.

Quilling

Central flower:

(make 4): 30 cm teardrops

(make 4): 40 cm teardrops

Quarter positions:

(make 2): 30 cm teardrops

(make 2): 20 cm teardrops

Heart scrolls (make 4): 15 cm

Scrolls:

(make 28): using 7.5 cm

(make 8): using 5 cm

To assemble

❋ Using the quilling board markings to guide you, position the central flower.

❋ Place a small dot of glue under the rounded end of the quarter-position teardrops, and place them as on the diagram, just inside the marked oval.

❋ Apply glue to pinched end of heart scrolls, and push between petals of central flower as shown. Allow to dry. Place a dot of glue where heart scrolls touch outer teardrops, and secure in place.

❋ Each quarter of the lid is now filled with scrolls—7 x 7.5 cm and 2 x 5 cm per quarter. Start at the heart scrolls, and work in. Attach one scroll at a time, applying glue to straight end, pushing between petals of central flower, and allowing to dry. Place a dot of glue on previous scroll/s and push new scroll into place, allow to dry. The 5 cm scrolls are the last to be positioned—see diagram for placement.

❋ Allow completed design to dry for at least 24 hours, then apply at least two coats of gold spray paint. Don't be heavy-handed—several thin coats are better than risking 'runs' of thick paint. You will need to turn the design over and give at least one coat from the back if you are to get into all the hidden corners. Again, you may like to give a final coat of varnish for protection.

❋ When completely dry, use an art brush to paint the back of the quilling sparingly with glue, invert and place in middle of lid.

Gold trinket box

15mm: ¹/₁₆"; 3mm: ¹/₈"; 6mm: ¹/₄"; 9mm: ³/₈"; 12mm: 1"; 15mm: ⁵/₈"; 20mm: ³/₄"; 25mm: 1"; 30mm: 1¹/₄"; 40mm: 1⁵/₈"